to (Gay)

It's all about

we mad

Matthew

xxx

Edited By **matthew michael taylor** With **Darren Gray**

now that's what i call
Monkey Kettle

vol.1 1999-2004

First published in the United Kingdom by Next Century Books Limited, 2005

Next Century Books Limited
P.O. Box 6113
Leighton Buzzard
Bedfordshire
ENGLAND, LU7 0UW

www.nextcenturybooks.com

Design & Layout :
Jason Purcell - www.funkbuddha.co.uk

Cover Painting :
James Türl

Printed & Bound in India by Gopsons

A CIP catalogue record for this title is available from the British Library

ISBN 0-9544011-8-2

DEDICATION

for all the staff at Monkey Kettle Towers, past and present:
Jim, Diane, Simon, Simon, Helen.

with thanks to DG for his enthusiasm and support throughout
this project, Tim at NCB, Jay at Funkbuddha and to C, C & E
for the unflinching backing, and Romantic-era-style patronage,

and many soft kisses to all the MK Arts playas who have backed
us over the years; Steve, David, Tony & Carolyn, Sammy J, Sue
Q and all at MADCAP, Zahida and the MK Community Foundation,
Guy and all at MK Arts, and anyone else we've forgotten,

to all the poets, writers and artists who have appeared in
Monkey Kettle past and present,

and a billion vodka and cokes raised to all the many mini
monkeys.

I always promised meself I'd dedicate me first book to me mam
and dad. I dunno if this counts, but here it is anyway.

MMT2005.

CONTENTS

Blue

Red

Green

Pink

Black

INTRODUCTION

I have to admit, I never really thought it would get this far.

The story of how I suddenly turned to the sleeping girl beside me one sunny Summer morn in 1999, and said "hang on – why don't I start my OWN poetry magazine?" is one I didn't think I would still be re-telling six years later. I'm not normally known for carrying out my harebrained schemes, you see.

But it made a lot of sense at the time. If I started my OWN poetry magazine, I could celebrate all the talents of my friends and associates, the first generation to actually be born and grow up in and around Milton Keynes. As a city (in all but name) yet to even reach it's fortieth birthday, culture has been slow yet steady in developing here - but we knew it was there, and so attempting to compile some of it into a low-budget "poetry and stuff" magazine seemed a good way to go. Plus I could put my own poems in it, no questions asked!

However, if we'd just launched the magazine and then only managed to include and sell it among our own group of arts & lit peers, it would have never got past issue #2. It's been the enthusiasm and support of people we don't know, both in MK and further afield, which has kept us in the game so long, and kept us growing and improving as we've gone on.

Monkey Kettle has never been, and will never be, about being the best poetry magazine in the country. But that's not as important to us as being honest, enthusiastic, experimental, and supporting new and inexperienced talent alongside more polished practitioners of the printed word.

So, what have we here, then? Well, this anthology covers the first 20 issues of Monkey Kettle, from the frankly quite patchy first issue way back in the Autumn of 1999, to the triumphal fifth birthday issue #20 released late on in 2004. We've carefully selected the poems and prose here enclosed, both as Monkey Kettle staff, and through a public vote, conducted in 2004. Hopefully all your favourites are here – we've certainly tried to get a good mix of the regular Monkey Kettle names and faces alongside writers from stranger borders.

Obviously some pieces we've included in the magazine would be too long to reproduce here, such as Cissy Aeon's superlative series "Soap Stories", or her novella "The Screaming Of Milotchka Stitch" (published by Monkey Kettle Press, and still available to buy from **http://www.monkeykettle.co.uk/mkpress.htm** of course!). And some of the poets in earlier issues have been impossible to track down to ask for permission, but on the whole we think this compilation gives an accurate picture of the vim and vigour of each issue of Monkey Kettle, only freshly wrapped in posh ISBN-laden surrounds!

Perhaps this would be a good time to give a brief pencil-line drawing of the full history of Monkey Kettle. After the initial idea in bed, we launched the first issue of the magazine on National Poetry Day, October 1999, upstairs in the Library, Central Milton Keynes. A few people turned up, I sat nervously on a chair with Simon on the floor next to me, and lo – Monkey Kettle was come among the world.

The first issue, as I've said, is not brilliant, although it contains an embryonic blueprint for the sights to come – poems by talented local writers mixed together with work from further afield. In issue #1, that was pretty much confined to Susana Meza, a pen-pal I'd somehow made in Venezuela that summer. Still, from tiny acorns etc.

Clearly, though, we were going to need to tell a few more people about the magazine for it to grow and improve. I opened us up a PO Box so people could send us submissions, and went onto as many poetry websites as I could find, adding our details. Slowly, surely, we started getting submissions from outside MK, and what's more, some of them were excellent! The inclusion of writers like Paul Rafferty, Cissy Aeon, Richard Zola and Jon Oyster in that first year enabled us to add a completely new dimension to our ever-more-confident stammerings.

From the start, what seemed to make the magazine popular locally was the inclusion of other things than just poetry – the regular "Young Poet And His Pals Visit..." section saw us travel the highways and byways of Milton Keynes documenting what we saw, and the "Monkey Kettle Has Been Eating" section allowed us to big up all the things we'd been experiencing during the compilation of each issue. Both of these have remained favourites of our regular readers, and examples of both have been included in this anthology.

By the summer of 2000, we were determined to raise our profile locally, especially as the quality of the mag was improving. To this end, we made up a short, free issue (the much-sought-after Issue #3.5) and gave it out at the local music festivals (MK has an excellent run every June, "Folk On The Green", "Togfest" and "The Waterside" – all are highly recommended if you're round these parts!)

A more important step also came that summer when I discovered that you can send copies of your magazine to the National Poetry Library on the South Bank, and they'll display it in their excellent Magazines section. Many's the time I've passed a happy afternoon reading and researching in there, and I'm always proud to see Monkey Kettle displayed among the other myriad offerings from the length and breadth of the UK. Compared to other magazines, we're often a bit cheap-looking, but our cover price of just £1 reflects that, and in fact reading many of the other mags, I like to think we more than match them for quality as well as offering value for money and a cheerful DIY ethic!

Our local profile raised even more from issue #6 onwards, though, as we struck a deal with the new Ottakars bookstore which had opened in the Midsummer Place shopping centre. They would stock Monkey Kettle, taking none of the profits, in return for some advertising of author events in our pages, which we were more than happy to do. I still have the first issue ever sold in a legitimate retail outlet, receipt stapled proudly to it!

Another turning point. We also struck deals with Athena (at least while Diane still managed it!), and later the local antique bookshop, Periplus Books in Stony Stratford. Ottakars also allowed us to use their coffee shop to launch issue #7, which was good fun, also being notable for the first time we met extremely regular and long-term contributor *Caz* Wolfson and her pal Bunny.

Now it seemed definite that the magazine was going to work as a plan, we decided it was high time to get ourselves a website. With some funding help from Milton Keynes Arts Association (who have regularly supported us over the years, including in the production of this book!), we opened up **http://www.monkeykettle.co.uk/** in April 2001, a regularly mixed bag of articles, reviews, links, pictures, and occasionally even poetry! Getting on for four years later, we've had well over 10,000 hits, and are about to embark on a total revamp (fingers crossed!)

By issue #10, it was clear we were here to stay – we made that one a bumper issue, including work from several continents, and our profile was such that we even adorned the cover of the MK Citizen (widely-read local paper) What's On section. The photo showed me, Simon and James sat in our spare room in Conniburrow, which I'd bedecked with old issues of Monkey Kettle to make it look like some sort of weird shrine. We're all looking at copies of the mag, while behind us looms the super-imposed head of one of James' many toy monkeys. He looks a bit like some kind of simian overlord. It's a funny picture.

In March of 2002, somehow we also managed to swing an appearance on an Anglian regional What's On programme ("The Biz"), being interviewed by Andrew Lynford, who you'll all remember as Gay Simon, Tiffany's brother in Eastenders. The programme went out at about half eleven at night on a Friday, as I recall, but was one of our greatest moments. Just after an advert for a gig by Dog Toffee in Colchester that weekend, (and some embarrassing shots of me reading a poem straight to camera in among a load of long grass) our interview started. As the caption "Matthew Michael Taylor" came up on the screen, Andrew waded in with his first question – "Matthew, a lot people find poetry inaccessible – why do you think this is?"

The other highlight: "I've got to ask – what happens at parties when people ask you what you do, and you say you're a poet?" Matthew: "Well, they think we're cool, immediately". Cut to side-shot of James laughing at me. Is the gap between my front teeth really that big? That's fame, I guess… Andrew promised to send us some of his own poetry. He never did.

We occasionally get national poets in Milton Keynes, and never miss an opportunity to set up a stall in the foyer at their events. Which is why John Hegley has twice held up issues of Monkey Kettle at his gigs, and why the legendary and godlike Roger McGough asked "how much does it cost?" (when told a quid, he quipped "what a rip-off!")

Issue #13, in the Autumn of 2002, broke new ground when we devoted an entire issue to poems, pictures and writing specifically about Milton Keynes. This took Fullers Slade, the Number 9 bus, and Downhead Park onto a national stage. Well, kind of. Maybe we'll try that again one day, it was good larks...

We've never really fitted into any categories for local awards (my persistent lobbying for a Best Poetry Magazine Award has always fallen on deaf ears), but we knew we'd really started to invade the local arts consciousness when James (who does almost all our covers) was nominated for the Best Milton Keynes Artist award, along with our sister theatre companies, at the 2003 MK Citizen GO! Awards. Our table was a lot drunker than the others, though – we've never really fitted in at that sort of friendly event, being a bit more in line with the nervous outsiders. Apart from Simon. And Diane.

In 2003, we decided it was all going so well that we'd like to branch out a bit. And lo, Monkey Kettle Press was born. Basically the chance to print longer works or specific collections in almost exactly the same format as the magazine, these standalone items have nonetheless proved equally as popular. Did I mention that you can still order them online? Oh, that was pages ago! Here's the address again - **http://www.monkeykettle.co.uk/mkpress.htm**

We've done four Monkey Kettle Press collections so far, including the ever-popular "Captain Gin" collection of Simon's work, and the novella by Cissy Aeon "The Screaming Of Milotchka Stitch", and we plan to do another couple this year, once we've had a bit of a rest from compiling this anthology, of course!

Over the last couple of years, Real Life(TM) has intruded occasionally into our late-twenty-something Monkey Kettle lives, but we've managed to stumble onwards, and hopefully the magazine has retained all its varying qualities throughout that time.

We've now managed to host two Monkey Kettle Art Exhibitions, one at the excellent MADCAP Theatre in the late summer of 2003, one at Stantonbury Campus in January 2005, and both have been brilliant experiences. We limit these exhibitions to people who have had their work appear in the pages of Monkey Kettle, and use them as a good excuse to show work which doesn't necessarily scan down to an A5 page of black and white very well! Just another excuse to branch out the empire, really...

And here we are... There's more literature in MK than when we started, which is exactly what we'd hoped would happen. Local reading and performance poetry groups like Scally-Rivers and Speakeasy allow writers from the city to interact and enjoy each other's work. We're even hearing rumours of other poetry magazines for the first time!

We've built up another generation of regular contributors from both home and away over the last couple of years (these things seem to go in two-year cycles, almost! I dunno what that sez about the lives of poets...), and the likes of Paul Grant, Anthony Kane Evans, Kit Bowman and Rogan Whitenails are helping us carry the torch on into our next five years.

Sometimes people ask me "what's your favourite thing about Monkey Kettle?" (no, really, they do!)

It's not tricky to answer, but I do have a few. I definitely like seeing the improvement of young writers who send us their first tentative murmurings, then, with just a bit of encouragement, develop into capable poets. This has happened quite a few times over the years, with writers like Lucy, Rachel, Andi, K T and *Caz*, and never fails to make me cheerful.

I also like the personal, DIY ethos of the magazine. Yes, we could probably try and get grants to get it printed glossily, and maybe one day we'll think about that, but at the moment we're happy with it having the personal touch. Certainly we've only risen to the ranks of Cult Poetry Magazine, but that's a niche we don't mind edging our way into in the slightest. Unlike some mags, we're quite happy to admit we've printed some rubbish in our time, and no doubt will do again! (Oh yes!) But we've also printed lots and lots of good stuff, and hopefully much of it is collected here for your reading pleasure...

I think my favourite thing about Monkey Kettle, ultimately, is that it's ours. In a world where we have to sit at desks for much of the time earning money to pay off all our debts, it's something They (whoever They may be) can't take away from us.

So, feel free to pull up a sofa or a barstool, furnish yourself with a cup of sugary tea or a nice pint of Kronenbourg 1664, and Get Involved. This book can either be read by flicking through and seeing where it falls open; by loosely grouped sections; or in standard left to right order. It's up to you. Or you could invent your own method, let us know.

Hope you enjoy it. Thanks for buying it, if you have. Rock on.

matthew michael taylor, editor.

MONKEY KETTLE : ART AND SCIENCE OVER BUSINESS AND MANAGEMENT

:BLUE

Sometimes, when it rains

Sometimes,
on those soft days,
when the rain drizzles light,
and the sky is full of greys,
and it feels like night.

I stop thinking.

Sometimes,
on those sunny days,
when all is bright,
and I feel the summer rays,
and the clouds are white.

I stop worrying.

Sometimes,
on those quiet days,
when our embrace is tight,
and it's enough to laze,
and it just feels right.

I start feeling.

but only sometimes.

Mike Cordell.

Disappeared

In one version of the story
he returns home to Ireland,
after a lifetime of hard
labour in England, to the bosom
of his family
In the other version he is prone
to drink, so much so by age
forty four he is unable
to dry out. Instead he walks
the endless streets, looking
for a quiet place to lie down and sleep
In a final version, he finds work
in the docklands, but the quiet spaces
elude him. So one night after everyone
has gone home, he walks
out along the girders, pauses a moment
against the skyline before he disappears.

Caroline Davies.

So far under the sofa

So far under the sofa
I've discovered covers
For four flooring rings,
Marked "Two by Two"
To add to things.

And under the table, a ladle
Able to scoop soup
With many mini plastic sticks
And banned band bandages
Up to their "tooth hair" tricks.

All in all small wonder
So few true tasks complete
When a myriad of minutia
Distract tracts of time
While one wonders, wandering off one's feet.

Dave Stephenson.

At Home in Leeds

I can say "tara" and "hiya then"
With the best of them and "mi mam"
Comes naturally to my tongue as does
"Dies Irae", "Die Schőne Mullerin" and
Even "Τον οινοπν Ποντον" - Homer's wine -
Dark sea on a good day.

It's my home Leeds Nine and thereabouts
Of what's left of it, most of the roads
Go nowhere, the bus stop by Bridgewater
Place must be the loneliest in Leeds.

"Where on earth have you been ?"
A London friend asked on the phone,
"Playing out on the Hollows with Margaret",
I answered to her amazement, "We play there
Every day, I suppose are clothes get mucky
But are mams'll not much mind."

I can even find a new walk, by the side of Cook's
Moor End Works, a path past an empty factory
By a railway spur unused since before the war -
I'm going to go on about the neglect to the
Council's Path Preservation Officer, who's as
Mad as me - Imagine, getting paid for poetry !

This rusting railway's worth a mint in verse
Brilliant yellow chickweed growing through
The clinker, real wood sleepers rotted to a turn -
I must inform Bradford University's Tutor in
Yorkshire Transport Archaeology for his conceptual
Analysis in accepted terminology.

The path ends suddenly by Middleton Light Railway
But I don't relish restoration - give me genuine decay
Any day.

There must be a god of railways, who cares
As I do for their rusted railings and spike -
Topped crossing gates. I'd have a gang of
Irish navvies dig out the gates from where
They've stuck and haul them across the road
To hold the traffic up while we get up steam
In 'John Blenkinsop'. The levers for the points
And the great brass wheel beside them have not moved
For fifty years; the last time I tried to turn them
I was with Margaret going to Hunslet Feast and
She was ten and I was twelve.

Barry Tebb.

Broadwell
Windmill

Chrissie Williamson.

Again upon return

absence
makes my eyes widen
when we touch
your blue cotton
against my yellow
tanned arms on pale
soft entangled limbs
as if again for the first time
heartbeats fast in anticipation

Caz Wolfson.

chameleons

1:

the day bursts softly like a bubble above my head and i open
my eyes. i am seven storeys up and sleep-drunk, high under
the covers. an aeroplane crawls across my window. i move
nothing except my eyes.

the room is full of chameleons. you can't see them, of course,
and they're not pets. they live here like the mice and the dust-
mites and me; little invisible dragons under the bed and on the
picture-rail, eyes swivelling everywhere in cool reptilian apathy.
they see everything i do and do not do and they have absolutely
nothing to say about any of it.

they're very discreet like that.

like them, the day is colourless. nothing but transparent sky
outside the window and snow the colour of white noise. what's
out there is of no concern to any of us. today is a day for living
amongst our dead skin. it is sloughed around and against the
legs of tables and chairs and it slouches in the bed. it covers
every available surface in a barely visible sheen of passing time.
it coats Maria while she is still trapped and sleeping in my
arms. she isn't part of the day yet. her eyes, when they are
open and clear of sleepdust, will be brown as sugar. her creamy
hair is spilt and it oozes over her shoulders. she is sticky as
fly-paper. i can't let go of her. if you look around the room
you will find photos of us looking equally stuck.

i clean my teeth. i sense the chameleons move as bubbles
burst softly in my mouth. the South Downs water is chalky and
brisk and feels like a walk along the cliffs. i could jump in the
car and drive there now. i could slip my soft bonds. i could
pretend to be homesick for somewhere or lovesick for someone
else. seagulls would tail me and the deep snow would bite at
the soles of my boots and the east wind would blow epic postcard
epigrams into my ears like parting put-downs or famous last
words, so i could leave the world with airy levity, maybe dress
like a choirboy, sing or shout or sick up something sweet and
flimsy in my defence, insist on a urinal for my headstone, swim

like a jellyfish, sting like the sea, drown like a spider in the sink.

Maria sleeps with a tooth under her pillow. it fell out when she was five and the fairies have never taken it. she doesn't expect to wake up and find it gone anymore. maybe that's why she keeps leaving it.

under my pillow i keep a mouldy book with a crocodile-skin cover. inside is scattered an entire firmament of musical notes, held in constellations by bars and clefs and with each line footnoted by a muttering of Latin. in the margins are expletives and dirty drawings i made when i was twelve. i used to sing from this book. i hailed Mary so much she got sick of it and slept with me to shut me up.

2:
there's a girl who sits smoking in the pews. she comes to every rehearsal and lights up, despite the signs. she holds her smoking arm like the Queen waving or the way the little doll of Jesus does in the icons, with two fingers up in blessing. when she tips her ash onto the tiles she makes it look like a benediction.

the chameleons cluster around her. their gargoyle toes grip the back of her bench and one perches on her shoulder. they are not in the least interested in my performance. they just have to be here.

i'm one of many mouths identically dressed and tended. i'm a tenor now. those soft bubbles between my legs have dropped like conkers and there are fillings in my teeth. just a few months ago life was a beach: yellow sands and ribbony spray, summer bubbles and starfish. chameleons sunned themselves to stone on the rocks. they were like bodyguards and i hardly noticed them stare. but there's been a sea-change. the sky and the coral and the rock-pools and chameleons have lost colour, like they're pale with mistletoe poisoning.

there are caves under the cliffs, big mouths of seaweed and glittering salt. the acoustics are better than in church. i sing

28

church songs here, but i change the words to filthy ones and i sing much louder.

i've stolen a car and we're taking a bumpy ride together to the cliffs, just Maria and the chameleons and me, up where it's really remote and the snow hasn't been touched. the heater is blurring and the seas sounds like it's coming in through the grille. we get naked and wriggly on the icy leather seats. i tell her we'll drive up to London and live there one day and she says i could maybe get a job in a choir there and wouldn't it be wonderful if she could come and hear me sing in Westminster Abbey or St Paul's one day and i say yes. i say she could pretend every Ave Maria was for her: Ave Maria, dei plena gratia.

she tastes of smoke and skin-cream.

3:
i filch in the fridge and drink the last of our milk. it clashes with the taste of toothpaste and leaves a cold, oyster-slick coating in my throat. Maria says i look like a boy when i drink milk. she says i only drink it as a comfort. she doesn't seem to realise she looks like a little girl when she's in the bath, a little pearl, and that the soapy bubbles are just as much of a comfort. she's always scrubbing herself of dead skin and getting younger. i tell her i prefer to concentrate on my bones.

among all the tiny rituals and habits that have attached themselves to us like limpets over the years, i have only one that i keep invisible from Maria. most mornings i have pupils whom i have to scrape through scales and other singing exercises, but on the days that i don't, i get up early and steal the tooth from under her pillow. i drive away, leaving behind a dry and dusty flat and a transparent city, and i head to the sea. the church has been pulled down now but the caves are still under the cliffs. i spend the time singing my old dirty church songs and pissing in the rock-pools like i did when i was twelve. as always, the chameleons watch. they wait for me to do something wicked and sometimes i'm tempted. i never do because i've brought something with me that i have to return.

Maria doesn't expect to wake up and find her little tooth gone. and so far she hasn't. on the morning that she does, i couldn't say what she'll do.

Cissy Aeon.

Memory 1: Looking for Wendy

Hiding greens under mashed potato:
a scooped-out, semi-solid mountain.
Cold, hard cubes
hid a myriad of poisons:
cabbage, runner beans, death.

Marcus Richards took a tyre
to the top of the climbing frame,
and stood, triumphant,
on top of our world.

A sea of awe-struck faces lapped at its legs,
Astounded.

The only black kid in our school.

Six and a half years for attempted murder,
but I still see him with that tyre;
Godlike.

And the girl with the lank hair,
who cried every day,
and who no-one bothered to ask
or learn her name.

Sentenced to the Wendy house one morning,
For speaking in mind;
I read in stillness
And looked for Wendy
Through the shuttered windows.

I never found her.

Matt Gambrill.

Bone Lady

She'd had many lovers who inevitably
Let her down and always broke her heart,
But she was not bitter and thought it best
Just to move on and not to keep their letters
Because they made her weep and all the clothes
And presents she gave away to charity shops just
So she could sleep. It was just the bones she kept.
In every drawer and cupboard, on shelves and corners,
Under tables and in sinks and baths and cisterns,
In wardrobes and chests, in boxes and baskets.
She kept them, not in any order, not chronologically,
Not by size or by weight, not by hair colour, or eye colour
Not by status or wealth, but she knew every bone
Be it a long strong thigh bone, or a small brittle ear bone
There were jawbones and shoulder bones, leg bones
Breastbones and arm bones, rib bones and hipbones
Fingers bones and toe bones and of course the gleaming
Row of skull bones smiling at her from the mantel shelf
And in her pink and chintz bedroom in a jewellery box
A collection of small delicate vertebrae shattered
Just at the moment of death.

David Gildner.

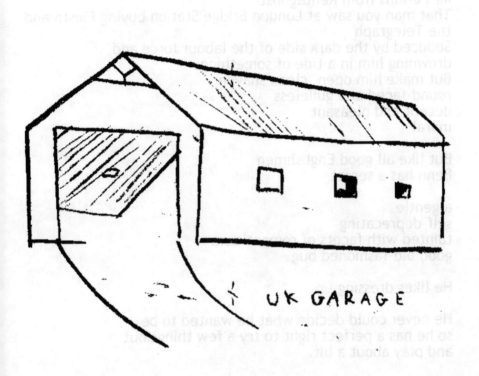

Steve Groom.

The Shopkeeper asks...

Anyone remember Mr Benn?
If you've not met then try to imagine an everyman of sorts.
Homely, shiny-faced,
suited and bowlered.
Chas Smash in the Cardiac Arrest video
Mr Perkins from Rentaghost
That man you saw at London Bridge Station buying Fiesta and
the Telegraph
Seduced by the dark side of the labour force and
drowning him in a tide of something.
But make him open, clean shaven
round-faced and guileless
decent and pleasant
moral

But like all good Englishmen
Benn has a secret

a gentle
self-deprecating
tainted with facets of romanticism
good old-fashioned bug

He likes dressing up.

He never could decide what he wanted to be
so he has a perfect right to try a few things out
and play about a bit.

And like all good Englishmen
he plays discreetly
in a quiet little shop
at the weekend
or Friday after work.

He's been
A clown
A caveman
A chef

A chauffeur
A spaceman
A knight in shining orange cardboard armour

But like all good Englishmen
he couldn't keep it all to himself

and now They know
and They are coming for him
so he's hiding under the table in just vest, pants, socks
and bowler.
Keeping out of the sun
Flicking V's through closed curtains

Lee Nelson.

Love on a cold planet

hold me on Neptune, take me to Venus
fly me past planets with nothing between us
show me the stars with the twinkly features
hide us behind them where no-one can reach us
cry me a stream where we'll float bits of tissue
a warm, moonlit place where I'll no longer miss you
where we can look out as a thousand suns set
   and kiss me my love on my cheeks that are wet

Andy Pearson.

Unlike That Summer When I Thought About You All The Time

Always make your bed
Even if your room is a mess
always make your bed
holding your head
hangover I must confess
I may be a mess
But I always make my bed

Always make your bed
I think about you less (now)
I always make my bed
I'm cleaned and fed
(under duress)
I'm crossed and blessed
I always make my bed.

Keith Crawford.

"computers for schools"

at work they started doing those vouchers again
and they come in badly-glued books
backed by little cardboard rectangles
which i've been collecting
i don't know why

sometimes i think that i'll create some vast landscape
pieced from cardboard oblongs
where i can walk and talk and laugh

sometimes i see myself writing little thoughts
or aphorisms
on them, and wiring them all up
so they dangle above my bed
to give me good dreams and inspiration

sometimes i see the great environmentalist
burying them in the back garden
[next to the grave he would have dug if he'd ever had a pet]
so they'll decompose
for a good reason
and return

that is important

when i've been thinking that
- rocking back and forward on my bed -
i slowly start to dream
as the tower of cardboard totters on my table
and then my eyelids slip open
and i see
wavering
the ghosts of the trees

Andi Thomas.

.... watch her little gestures ....

don't it make you sad,
 to know that no one,
hears a word you say,
the uncanny, clear as air,
 sadness and dismay.
look at me,
 you must see,
aren't i SO,
 like certain things,
banned from t.v.
 how could anybody,
miss this sadness
 that surrounds me everyday.
am i reminding you,
 of anyone at all,
doesn't it strike,
 you as some one we knew,
look at me,
 do you see it now?
the very image of,
 someone's cigarette,
burnt out and discarded,
 eyes with no expression,
this is me,
now do you see?
how could anybody miss?
on this beautiful day,
it's so obvious,
i'm half burnt out.

KT.

39

The Caudal Appendage and Haemorrhoids

(tried a hot bath, more fibre, taking my overdue books back to the library. Nothing has worked, and it's been two days now ...)

Oh, "where the sun don't shine" -
Overdue, and a terrible fine!
Avoid all haemorrhoidal bleeding -
Take your books back after reading;
Take them back, renew your loan!

A lump emerged, as big as the bone
That protrudes at the base of my spine,
Rendering me supine,
With knees aloft, wide apart,
And now it hurts to fart -
More than hitherto known;
A lump as big as my tailbone -
With blood, so bright, almost pink;
A lump the size of the missing link -
The size of the bone where a primate's tail
Had tethered itself to a hay bale,
Rather than climb
Beyond the time
When we evolved and borrowed books.
The monkey's hay bale looks
So comfortable in my mind
(My books were late and I was fined),
Extinction's healing void
Would surely soothe my haemorrhoid
(Dodos flying, never landing,
Library fines are still outstanding) ...

If I sat on extinction's bale,
I know that, soon, like the tail
That evolution docked,
My coccyx - usually easily knocked,
Usually sour and petrified,
And routinely made to hide

Beneath my pants, under a label –
Would loosen and be able
To swish and ripple gracefully ...
Let something else evolve, not me:
A bookish, thrombotic droid,
Emerging in time, like a haemorrhoid -
Straddling the dolphin's fin.
Insert a finger, pop me back in:
Let me sit on this bale -
My brain like the bone where a primate's tail
Once wagged,
As its hands dragged
On the floor;
Leave me behind, my bottom is sore.

With a stern "shush!" in the Reading Room,
I see another haemorrhoid loom,
Like a comet, with a tail of sparks,
And the mildew of studious bite marks
On the plastic arms of my glasses,
Glistens beneath my hair, as it passes:
I study for what - a Distinction?
And all I crave is extinction ...

Make me endangered, then make me gone;
The tail I had, like the neck of a swan,
Fell on its wings, grew shorter,
Then dived for something under the water –
Extended deep, then dissolved;
And so my body evolved
Without a tail – without grace –
And now I feel compelled to chase
Another morsel of sinking bread:
Let me dissolve in the river bed;
No more a biped, nor erect,
No longer sore, no longer pecked
By my coccyx, madly,
Under a label, cut out badly,
So the jagged washing instructions remain
To prickle and scratch ... oh, let me crane
My neck to chase the sinking bread:
Let me dissolve in the river bed.

The bale looks soft, but might its hay
Scratch me in a similar way
To how the label does now?
I crave extinction, but exactly how,
Where I sit – and what on –
Will make the difference when I am gone:
Luxuriously extinct –
When my tender coccyx has slinked
Away from the base of my spine,
I will find a comfortable place to recline ...

Endangered, in limbo, extinct, limber!
Felling the fins of sharks – timber!
I kneel in the path of the toppling fin,
Hoping the impact will pop me back in –
As the fin spanks my rear end;
Where the fin had stood, light will descend
And seedling fish will thrive.

Oh, why did my tail not survive?
Ka Cox, the girlfriend of Rupert Brooke,
Had a coccyx that people mistook
For a tail – it hung so loosely;
And while she secretly prayed profusely
That her tail would someday shrivel, the poet
Secretly wished his muse could grow it,
For he knew its power;
And he climbed to the top of the library tower
In Cambridge, by the River Cam,
And shouted to Ka: "From where I am,
I can see the tails in the city of Ely,
But none are as loose, none swish freely –
They climb the cathedral like vines!"
He returned his books and paid his fines ...
Gotta go kak, got gut rot!
The vicarious kicks,
That he got
From Ka Cox's coccyx,
Are in taste quite poor –
Leave me behind, my bottom is sore.

A shower curtain of sharks,

A tea cosy T-Rex;
The mildew of studious bite marks
On the plastic arms of my specs,
Glistens beneath my hair - shines through;
And the ice axe, placed adjacent to
The Yeti's footprint, for scale,
Was once a twirling, limber tail ...
But no more.
Leave me behind, my bottom is sore.

So flimsy now, without their fins,
A shower curtain of sharks begins
To hug my back, as I stay kneeling –
Its clinging transparency revealing
The gargoyle of my coccyx, behind.
Naked and shampoo-blind,
I long to hear the clatter of rings
Sliding along, as extinction slings
The shower curtain aside;
And the ligature applied
To my haemorrhoid - tied tightly -
Would also be used to strangle me,
And when we drop off, the world will be raw ...
Leave me behind, my bottom is sore.

Where the sun don't shine, it will set,
And black salubrious sweat
Will flow again, beneath the pleats
In my anus; and Keats
Should have made the distinction:
"Fully in love with easeful extinction
Is greater than half, with death, it seems ... "
Tell me the meanings of my dreams,
And why Darwin and Freud –
So anally retentive –
Never pondered the haemorrhoid:
How it provides an incentive
To be extinct;
For these two factors are linked,
Like the coccyx and the tail ...
An ode to Florence Nightingale -
The wounded in war;

Leave me behind, my bottom is sore.

Rogan Whitenails.

Diane Hainsworth.

45

'Venice'

Turn the pages of abstract
I will learn to solder
My own synapses
Feelemotionlike a blunt end
Again, and then wash my hands.
Now Wash Your Hands.
I only see moments, blips
And. Quiet, now.
Of how it could be if I could just keep down my pride.
Along with all that liquor.
And spiked shadows
Of chandeliers in plastic blue celebration
Tell me to stop and sleep
And listen to the taxi drunk night noises
And smell the comfort smoke.

Rachel George.

Child-space

Hyperion. Hyperspace. Housing redevelopment scheme.
Quasar. Quasi-space. Quick changes make them scream.
Children on the bus
Children on the floor
Children playing in the garden of the girl next door.
We do what they tell us to
We do what they say
Growing up a gradient every single day.

Aggravated vehicle theft. Grievous bodily harm.
Assault upon a citizen - who's to say what's right and wrong.
Children in the playground
Children have a smoke
Children growing up too fast but can't be bothered to change.

Silicon. Cyberspace. Sex on the beach.
Coppers. Run away. Safety's out of reach.
Children on the dance floor
Children cannot cope
Children in a darkened corner learning how to grope
We see what they want us to
We know how to fly
Forget the truth we taught ourselves
And learn to live the lie.

Hyperion. Hyperspace.
Quasar. Quasi-space.
Silicon. Cyberspace.
Make a move - no more space
Children of today.

Wayne Miller.

run on

out not in
with the crowd
alone days
nowhere to hide
or run
away
tied by what is
Right
[no turning left]
stay onsite
abide
don't fit
out: stick out
with those others (only a few)
feel safe
but never secure

Caz Wolfson.

Do not try to break rules of social convention, especially if you're lonely.

I went to a hideous mother and toddler group once.
I got sick
and tired
(bitter)
of the conventionality.

The conversations never strayed.
Husbands,
puking kids,
money,
housework
and fucking losing weight.

So when I mentioned the dead pig I saw caught in a weir,
that seemed like it was dancing to the time warp,
they paused for a while
cringed
and turned their backs.

And so,
Yes, the weather was shite.
Yes, my baby kept me up during the night.
And yes, I was too fat for my height.

Charlie Satine.

THE YOUNG POET AND HIS PALS VISIT ... MK Archaeological Sites

Every issue or so, the young poet and one or more of his buddies take a road trip to a different estate in Milton Keynes. Their mission : - to experience all the sights, smells, sounds, and so on of the whole damn grid. If you would like to see The Young Poet (and his pals) visit your area, send nominations to the Monkey Kettle address. Ta. This one is from the Spring of 2002.

Me and Jim have been going to adult education courses, which has been illuminating to say the least. We enrolled on a ten week course in Archaeology at Stantonbury, and every Monday night we roll on down there and join our colleagues to learn about digging, dating, and periods of archaeological history. Smashing, it is.

And on a drizzly Saturday in March, we went on the first of our two "field trips". The second will be to Avebury in Wiltshire, the centre of Neolithic Britain (if you believe Julian Cope, anyway), but this one was around and about in our own fair city. One of the main jibes about Milton Keynes is it's newness, the fact that it's not many years older than we are – but this trip blew that lazy joke out of the water.

Our first stop, at Bancroft, is one of the more famous finds of ancient civilisation in MK, a Roman villa. This basically now consists of some wall foundations, which were added in the 19th Century to mark the original layout, but there are reconstructions of what it would have looked like on those helpful Heritage signs which accompany all journeys such as this.

Our tutor on the course, Martin, explained to us that the Romans had several villas in and around what is now Milton Keynes, particularly with Watling Street running through these fields. And the reason Watling Street is where it is, this far to the East, is apparently partially to do with the Iron Age hill fort we went to, way up in the Brickhill woods.

The Brickhill woods are marvellous anyway, the occasional

spectacular view across MK and North Bucks is worth a look alone ; but hidden up in the trees about quarter of an hour's walk in are the remains of a hill fort over two thousand years old. This takes the form of an overgrown trench and a slight raised mound running round the inside, and without knowing it was there, you'd just take it for deviations in the landscape. But this is ancient – the pre- Roman people that lived up there did so for some time, able to see for great distances in all directions, with less trees dominating the skyline.

That would have been ace, I reckon. To live at one with nature, high up on the hilltop, miles' worth of views stretching out at your feet. Obviously you wouldn't have been able to see the Theatre and the Snowdome back then, but still. Or have I just watched Watership Down too many times?

So there's a sense of history to be found, as long as you have somebody to show you where to look. Martin also took us to the abandoned medieval village just to the north of Old Wolverton, near the Galleon pub. The ruins of a motte and bailey castle slowly decay away into mud, while lines and dips in the fields show where the old cart roads led, when the original village was, long before Wolverton and Stony Stratford were even a couple of huts.

We've already been back there a few times since, Simon took his metal detector and found an old horseshoe. Tony Robinson eat your heart out.

In Woolstone there are the remains of an medieval fishpond system, also accompanied by a Heritage board reconstruction, and way out in Tattenhoe, we were shown the remains of an old moated grange next to the old but well-preserved church. Smashing.

Maybe our class think us odd, two blokes in their mid-twenties sitting among the Time Team devotees, but we had a brilliant day. Alright, we may have a been a bit hungover, and the main reason we survived through the day was some very explicit and vicious swearing when nobody else was listening, but still. Just to look past what you can see to what was once here is an interesting sensation. To feel a sense of the immense age of this soil, these rolling fields.

And I've started driving the couple of miles across North MK to Gino's, rather than using a more local van. We had a couple of kebabs from an outlet in Stacey Bushes, but they weren't the same, somehow. Not made with Gino's love, and not pre-empted by his urbane banter. Sigh. As James is wont to say, it all means summink, dunnit?

She Gave Me Water

The girl behind the bar
with long dark gypsy hair
tumbling over soft white skin
catches my eye and takes pity
ahead of all the others.

In that moment I become
Quasimodo falling helplessly
head over hump with
the beautiful Esmerelda
who despite his lack of looks
and social skills still gave him water.

David Gildner.

Sometimes I think too much, then Breath too much, Feel 2much

But other times I don't THINK enough, and don't Breath enough, and have no FEALing's at all.

I can go NUMB and Ignore REALITY, not Care at all,

Loose all SENSITIVITY.

But my thoughts co RACE around 4 days...., never making SenSe, causing CoNFUSiNG

ViLe Pains

Pains that leave me CoNFUSed and Weak. THEY WONT GO AWAY, I TRY.... I TRY!!!

I go NUMB, ignore REALITY, don't Care at all, loose all SENSITIVITY.

Why?

why can't I be like the others; they have problems, deal with them, Smile and **run to their MOTHERS,**

But I just dwell, think too much, Breath too much; feel 2much. Then I go NUMB, Now the world just doesn't want to know. so I RUN .... and I RUN; and run, till I come to the END, to the END of my MIND to the END!

And I turn around and PUT the END behind me,

And all of a SUDDEN; I find a cure;

The happiness that exists, The reason I am where I am 2DAY

THEN I JUST HOPE THE THE CONTENTEMENT should 4ever stay......, I pray.X

Amie-May.

54

God Lives in Bletchley

His real name isn't actually God,
it's Mike.
And contrary to popular belief, he's only fifty six.
Far from being omnipotent,
he actually feels quite disenfranchised and out of touch
with this modern world.
And his Tax returns confuse him.

I've seen God depicted as some benevolent
yet wrathful Santa Claus type guy.
Nothing could be further from the truth.
Mike is about 5ft 7,
wears a tatty corduroy jacket
and he's going bald.

I go round quite often, I think he's lonely.
He tells me about his time growing up in Cleethorpes.
I ask him important questions like "Why are we here?" and
"Why do you let bad things happen to nice people?"
He usually just looks confused.

Which I suppose has been the reaction
of ineffable supreme beings
since man first started to query the
day to day running of the universe.

I've spoken with Christians.
They tell me I need to open myself,
and let God into my heart.
I reply that I don't mind visiting the old coot,
but we're not that close.

They tell me he's everywhere,
to which I solemnly respond
that actually he's pretty house bound since the hip operation.
I offer to introduce them but they generally decline.

One suspects they have too much
respect for his magnificence,

55

or maybe they just don't like Bletchley.

Mike's got a pretty dark past.
We read about what he did to his son, in middle school.
I think I'm going to
ask him about all that soon,
but not quite yet.

Sometimes, on my way home from work
I can see him working his allotment.
In some ways, it's sad.
God, starting again from scratch
with peas and runner beans.

Did we really fuck this world up so bad?
Then again, its good to see -
an old man with green fingers,
still searching for perfect grace amongst the cabbages.

Simon Edwards.

Take me to your reader

Headquartered in Zargoid
Staple food beans
I arrived hearing Earthspeak
Disguised, Milton Keynes
I closely encountered
A church with a dome
A glass walled bright palace
I had to phone home
I gave up my freedom
I found me a bed
I placed my old paper
In a box that was red
Moated by water
I stuck to my orders
After sixteen long weeks
I began crossing borders
I developed strange markings
I soaked them in Dettol
I spoke to my masters
Through the Lord Monkey Kettle
But now they desert me...
Is anyone there?
Please spare twenty Groids
For my Rocket-ship fare

Andy Pearson.

1.

The rain persists.
Your image smeared by
Liquid uncontrollable.
Your image smears.

The scarred tissue realigns itself
Beside
What resides
At the forefront
And strikes,
Invited by a moment of effortless weakness,
To reoccupy
Me.

Me.
Your image smeared by streaming,
Steaming drops.
Your image smeared, smeared this way
That day.

        Noon.
To take away the veil
Your image smeared, so that you're
Image smeared no longer, after
Time.

        Time to tie the tightly huddled
And necessary
Into a bundle, with young yet yellowed string
And toss it...

But now,
      For now only,
          To the back.
Back, where it sits.
It sits behind, the scarred.
Scared.

The rain persists.

Tom Chapman.

M(ONKEY)
K(ETTLE)

12

the m(onkey) k(ettle) smoke
will bellow from the Big Boys

Sunday: A Sofa, 2 a.m.

You cling to my chest,
limpet-like, curled,
and palpitate gently
with damp heat.

Lips slightly parted,
lungs pushing softly –
a first-aid dummy
fallen out of its cupboard.

Moonlight strokes a crisp
highlight on your forehead,
which frowns in a hieroglyph
of worried dreams.

You tuck yourself in under
my warmth, but I have
to shut my eyes on your
chicken-fillet cheeks.

You are not the one.

J C H Potts.

:RED

the two-finger cha cha cha

searching for a motive
a step-by-step guide to
Doing Well
once upon a Good-Girl time
I would've cared
hard-core Apathy reigns
Anarchy in the Classroom
"really, at your age..."
yes I should know better
www.don'tgiveafuck.com
scowl with an attitude problem
shrugs made of stone
I don't care anymore
where has the -real- me gone?
back in the real world
(don't know, don't care)
I stare at you: blank
if looks could kill...
I can't get to grips
with your bound'ries - I cross them
I don't see the problem, there's a
Rebel in Me
Devil in Me
don't like it? go on -
sue me

Caz Wolfson.

I Failed to Find An English Newspaper Anywhere

America has no care for the rest of the world
has no need for the rest of the world
And my home
with its pride and self-mockery
remains timeless
across deserts and plains
forests
smog and ocean

My home in amber
golden in memory
waiting to awake upon my return

America knows little of the rest of the world
little of its needs and calling
And my home
with its pain and its beauty
remains in another space
across history and religion
colour
rumour and truth

My home is golden
precious in its rarity
lies to the East in another day

America has no feeling for the rest of the world has no passion
for the rest of
    the world
It is a home
of beauty and many wonders
remaining distant
wide in nature and man
opportunity
fear and hope

My home for a while

America the Glorious
is a world to itself

America thinks it is the world
America knows so little   *Las Vegas Airport 11/8/02*

Darren Gray.

When Only A Fuck Will Do

I'm blunt and I'm frank
And a cunt is a cunt
And a wank is a wank,
But there's times, like,
You know man, there's times like,
When only a fuck will do?

Fuck this,
Fuck that,
This is fucking tall,
That is fucking small,
Who the fuck are you?
Who the fuck am I?
Don't really give a fuck,
He's a fucker,
She's a fucker,
Motherfucker,
I'd still fuck her,
I was fucked,
I fucked up,
I was really fucking fucked,
I was only fucking about,
Fucking around,
For fucksake,
I wanted to fuck you.

Jon Oyster.

Savoy Crescent
(from "The Not Quite Album")

Dancing round the cobbles
Drinking in the bars
Every month a new one
So we don't know where we are
Ten pints in the summer
Cuz the weather's oh so pleasant
You looking for a kicking?
Let's do the Savoy Crescent

Drinking beer from bottles
Wailing karaoke
In the Rat & Parrot
Lashed and feeling cokey
I'm not supposed to drink
On these cheap anti-depressants
What you looking at?
Let's do the Savoy Crescent

Kicked out of the Hog's Head
For smashing some twat's glass
We'll piss off to Bar Central
Get in, no questions asked
The music's guitar rubbish
You fuckin Indie peasants
Put on some fuckin hardcore
And we'll do the Savoy Crescent

Piss behind the Theatre
Spew up your kebab
Stumble to the Snowdome
Try to get a Raffles cab
I'm a fuckin big man
I'm a fuckin adolescent
Your mate looks like a queer
Fuck yeah, let's do the Savoy Crescent

matthew michael taylor.

Upon walking into a biker pub, seeing 3 really huge women who all thought they looked like super models, dressed in very tight leggings & even tighter Guns'n'Roses T-shirts

Take me down to Cellulite City
Where the grass is green
And the girls are
Fat

Paul Rafferty.

Pumpkin Jim

LARD.

sunday best

there's plastic on the church windows
to help protect their virtue
from the troubled teenagers
who find comfort in throwing bricks
here comes that girl again
she's always walking around
smoking streams of cigarettes
and spitting on the ground
the pensioners take it personally
while they're out walking the dog
exchanging saintly whispers as she passes
up to her usual tricks
they liked it better in their day
because it belonged to them
well, now they're strung out like the rest
queuing at the co-op, dressed in their sunday best.

K T.

See You In September

See you in September
words degrade and sentences fragment
ranting at my sunburn
and the scar tissue on my inner thighs
I don't have to imagine how it got there.

Why don't I have a degree?
IQ of 156 and a neanderthal
because I didn't blow three years
fucking lecturers and talking about God.

I went to sea and talked to God.
God said "I liked you better in black."
Very black, like the sunshine,
hide out in the open and always kill the messenger.

My sunburn highlights and conceals
What I am hiding in my backbone.
I fucked God and my lecturers
in one year. I'll see you in September.

Keith Crawford.

M.K.
(cheers to Betjeman)

Fall, friendly bombs on concrete cow,
no need for grass or grazing now...
We may as well all move to Slough,
fake bovine, death.

Come bombs, and scatter all about,
the damned incessant roundabout,
glass shops, glass roof, blow all glass out,
glass town, glass breath.

Mess up this mess called grid systems,
flat roofed houses, council rooms,
our little sub-suburban tombs,
of which we're proud.

And get the damned shell-suited hordes,
who circle round this city's wards,
in stupidly souped-up old Fords,
their music loud.

And smash statue of polished chrome,
its Möbius loop on granite stone,
reminding us that we're alone
with mirrored gloating.

But spare the lank haired, morbid poet,
the clown, the druid, here below it,
art neglects the hand that sows it,
Their minds are floating.

It's not their fault they cannot see,
this beauty wrought from purity,
in glass and girders endlessly,
reflected grace.

Who walk the veins of city red,
behemoth slug of tin and lead,
Its walls alive but soulless, dead,

Oh ashen face.

In prefab lofts, they gaze so far,
in club and pub and coffee bar,
to grasp this concrete abattoir,
in prose and lies.

Fall, friendly bombs on concrete cow,
who worries not for grass or plough,
they sit maybe forgotten now
beneath glass eyes.

Simon Edwards.

Once, twice.

She knew
the decision
had been
made for her
when blood
like red wine
was slowly
     absorbed
by the rug.

Neil Campbell.

Everything points to coal

You came at me
all teeth
looking for somewhere
soft
to take a bite
outta me

Ah but you know
better

After all this time
with you
I don't have any
soft places
Left.

Paul Grant.

False Advertising

a yellow Metro bus proclaims:
    WE ♥ MK
                how wrong could they be?
only Business loves MK
hear it from me
    WE ♥ 2H8MK
a processed town (haha, we couldn't even get city status)
complete with monumental graffiti-cows
subways depicting charming references
       to our sex lives. (don't you know we all suck cock?)
before-school addicts
take their last drag
then sulk into an infected education

no individual estates,
    all are programmed and unsafe
take a trip "up city"
and spend a fortune on a skimpy costume
to be worn with serious incriminations in mind

go anywhere you like; it's all the same
house, house, road, house, roundabout, roundabout,
roundabout...

MK has no history
    the future: to build an overwhelming mass of
                     processed houses
but still with yellow Metro buses speaking for the people:

WE ♥ MK

Caz Wolfson.

Beachampton

by Chrissie

Chrissie Williamson.

78

Me And the Major

Son
I'm your father
That much is true
But it don't matter
If you don't love me
I can always make more of you

James Türl.

Tripping over a dog whilst looking at the ground

Concrete.
FUCK!
Pavement Pig.

James Türl.

last words to salome

i
so not if at all
always

ii
you didn't say
you do not do
you didn't do
what you didn't say
so kept your promise
jealously locked away

iii
you're not you
nor a shoe
well-heeled is so
shoddy to anything
[-] barefooted
up bark-feet!
I yap

iv
what do you mean
sending minced words
love, we're due
for the fine chop

v
oh so infinitely pained
that everything's too bad for you
I couldn't stay
I couldn't say
why for art
must stand alone
need none,

depending on
everyone totally

vi
i cannot say
woman's words
for woman's ways
(and mine are still unspeakable
spite of these and your eyes)
head on a plate
gibbering its body back
your
stark
raving
body

vii
two-armed beast
one-backed bandit
someone else's
words you
might have said
I grow the new head
stocking-bag of seeds
salome gave
maniac eyes
brainiac figures
ammoniac sal

viii
so what if at all
anything? left
we too can stand
together but
I always
have
to be
wrong

ix
in the end, so the end
what the, in the end,
downwind

x
I pull out the twisted phone cord
I leap out of bed to confront
the guy watching us from the swivel chair
oops, I'm afraid he's here in the same room with us
then we're all grizzled and unshaven
in the early morning air standing at the bar
and get in on it together in some horrible way of
taking from each other while pretending we're alone.

Andrew Shelley.

The Young Poet And His Pals Visit ... the MK Dons

From the latter half of their first season in MK, February 2004.

Those who know me will be aware I've been very pious and self-righteous about the move of Wimbledon FC to this fair city. "Club thievery" I have called it, and "Filthy soul stealers destroying football" is another.

Still, that didn't stop me from going with Keith to see them play his club, Nottingham Forest, when Fay won him tickets off the radio. My morals have never been that stringent.

T'was a blisteringly cold February evening, and I was impressed by just how busy the ole Hockey Stadium was – later, on Teletext, I read that over 6,000 people watched the match. Although over half of that was Forest fans, either in the packed Away End, or dispersed secretively amongst the Dons fans.

And just who ARE these Dons fans? Nouveaux football supporters, popping along of a Saturday afternoon to watch some semblance of The Beautiful Game, invented circa Euro 96? Disenfranchised fans of other clubs, having a look at the new boys who have appeared on their doorstep rather than shell out the cash to travel to see their own team?

Not that watching the MK Dons comes cheap – at around £30 a ticket to watch a team languishing at the bottom of the First Division with only half the points of the next team above them, you'd need to have a strong wallet to cope...

Typically, I missed the only goal of the game, I was buying Keith and meself cheeseburgers, but apparently it was quite good. Unfortunately, it came in the 10th minute, meaning there was still another 80+ minutes of tepid, nondescript footer left to sit through. Or rather, sit and stand through – as Keith was in his wheelchair, we'd been advised to watch the match from a small gravelly area in front of one of the home stands. Which was okay for Keith, but as there were no seats for friends of fans in wheelchairs, I had to either stand, lean against the stand, or sit on some of the makeshift steps as the match slowly unfolded.

Yet, strangely, as the match wore on, I found myself warming to the dreadful Dons. They weren't anywhere near as good as Forest, no worldbeaters themselves (sorry Keith!) ; but their brand of head-down running hopeless optimism stirred something inside me, too.

Looking around behind me at the stands, it was clear that a large proportion of the crowd were kids – maybe this was the new demographic I was trying to ascertain. And maybe, too, this was a necessary perdition – to somehow gain the right to play here, this club, loved by others far away, must go through an awful soul-destroying stripping of talent, soul, hope, only to re-emerge the other side as a new club – as the MK Dons. And therein maybe lies salvation.

Or maybe that idea was something to do with Fay's thermos flask of "ribena-style warming health drink" which Keith had brought along. Who knows? Still, a few weeks later, West Ham beat Wimbledon 5-0, so I was happy, at least.

"Your ancestors were a bunch of tight-wearing thieves!", a big man shouted at the Nottingham Forest fans towards the end of the first half. Now that's a heckle!

um ah

um ah fucked him hard
um ah tub of lard
um ah no memory
um ah where's the chemist
AGAIN
UM AH

Charlie Satine.

Made of Mud

Everything started when the three of us were about.
Real reputation we had. Kenny was the lynchpin
so me & Rio were told: just leave this to me fellas
wait till I give ya a shout. We knew he couldn't get hurt,
and when some bull-faced blokes tried to wrestle him
he was slipperier than a bar of soap.

Slicker than most in his Burberry and Hilfiger and suchlike
Kenny was top dog.

Problems always came in the rain;
then he was as malleable as fine clay.
Kids'd press his nose in, stretch his ears
to Vulcan sized lobes, and his arms were pulled
so they became a nuisance for his knees.
It would take several hours of stretching and compressing
for me & Rio to mend him. Even then though,
there was something strange, the eyes weren't level,
the face too long. Everytime it was something different.
We couldn't blend the concaves up where he had a bump
with a cricket bat, and his stomach
was littered with indents from table-legs and fists
        and knives
from every fight we could think of.

On the night of the argument
we'd already had a few too many pints in town,
by the time we got back to Kenny's place and started
on the Triple X strength we were ready for some argy
but with just the three of us in the house
we started snapping at each other's faults.

Kenny said I was too quiet, never really joined in
any of the fights. I replied that Rio was the wuss
        of the pack
if anyone, to which Rio stood and said something like:
C'mon then ya couple of shit tongued wives – FIGHT.

Kenny took the mick saying Rio had limp wrists

and pretty boy lips. Then Rio's fist flew,
swung with that exaggerated shoulder fling
Carlsberg can produce. It grazed Kenny,
nothing worse than a pinch. His cheek blew inwards
like a gobstopper the wrong way out. A cheek
that went so far in he struggled to speak.

Mind you,
when I think back to it now, I'm sure those
    knuckles missed.

Julius Man.

Hyperbolic Protestation with Punky Climax

I'd rather
Bathe in bleach with a bison
Go the distance with Tyson
Read the entire works of Bill Bryson
Consume cow pats with flies on
French kiss a python
Befriend an electricity pylon
Sexually turn a crocodile on
I would sooner do all of these things
While wearing real live wasp rings
On my fingers
Than linger to watch
Top Of The Pops

1 2 3 4

FUCK OFF!

Jon Oyster.

Louise Fowler.

lost and lots of love

i mean, i was at quite a loose end
all things considered
locked out, and waiting
till you finished work
by half two i had sunk four pints
of Kronenbourg 1664, intent
over a discarded Mirror
in The Seven Feathers.

moving on to The Broken Gate
i had three double vodka and cokes
talking to an old Irish builder
with shaking hands.
on leaving i
felt more than
a little unsteady.

the thing to do, i surmised,
the most appropriate activity
under the circumstances,
was to visit Tolkien's grave
and see what that was like
so i walked down Five Mile Drive
muttering Sinitta lyrics
under my breath and spitting
into hedges.

it was quite an overcast day, you
might remember, and somewhere
on this quest i lost my pretend
nu-metal chain, which james gave me,
that used to be a lantern safety.

it took me a little while
to find the plot

but in the far end of the cemetery
in the Roman Catholic area
i noticed a group of people huddled

together around a stone.

shuffling closer in a way i believed
at the time to be a subtle one
but which in fact
included at least one headlong sprawl

i came to realise
that the Tolkien Society had
had the same idea.

they stood in mournful vigil
hands held, beards a-quiver
and spoke in whispered Elvish
a solemn reverent
elegy

the song of the Noldor
rose within me
like a flame
unwanted and unlooked for
and instinctively i responded

snapping a plank from a rotten bench
just beside me
and charging them, screaming
obscenities in the Undying Speech

i caught a professor of Norse mythology
a stern blow smack
across the forehead with artful precision
and proceeded to chase
his comrades away

meanwhile in the High Street McDonalds
the customers were getting restless
supplies of hot meat were getting low
and the teenage boys
behind the counter
looked nervous
as the grumbling
got louder

matthew michael taylor.

a shot of testosterone

haha
the tables are turned
and I am centre
look at me go
with vodka in my eyes
I stumble into
muscular surroundings
that I have not missed
but who catch me anyway
they are surprised
but no more than I
who attracts this attention
away from the flirtatious smiles
of my friends
maybe it's not all bad..

Caz Wolfson.

Killing Phase

You said that killing phrase the other day
"It doesn't matter"
In a tone so dead I thought
I thought
Well, it doesn't matter
Matter-of-fact
And why should it?
But even thinking that...
It could have been worse
I could have thought
"I don't care"
Which is worse than swearing
I swear
So I'll swear, grin and curse
Obverse to the killing phrases
The little assassins of passion
I'll breathe life through fire
And we'll laugh again,
Friends.
It's better to be frenzied
Than something that doesn't matter.

Faith Hope.

http://www.poem.com

http://www.the.com/ http://www.company.com/ ,
http://www.came.com/ http://www.and.com/ ,
http://www.bought.com/ http://www.our.com/ ,
http://www.words.com/

http://www.not.com/ http://www.even.com/ ,
http://www.the.com/ http://www.aardvark.com/ ,
http://www.was.com/ http://www.safe.com/ .

http://www.they.com http://www.even.com ,
http://www.bought.com/ http://www.the.com/ ,
http://www.useless.com/ http://www.ones.com/ ,
http://www.like.com/ http://www.snork.com/ .

http://www.simonedwards.com/

http://www.the.com/ http://www.bastards.com/
http://www.even.com/ http://www.bought.com/
http://www.my.com/ http://www.name.com/

Echolalia

Never any more . lonely
Never the mirrorkiddies
Sweet summer hooded gunman
    Red\eyes blackeyes shifting sand dunes mirrors in the
fingernailsBlisters on
the
    neckOverexposed and underdeveloped
Sheholdsherbreathandathousandthousandantscrawlacrossher
waitingchest
I Never really could sleep
More more redredeyes

Basilisk
If you look out of the window you can see where I parked the
car, darling
If you look under the car you can see the wheels
   Cockatrice
Where did I put those keys?
Can I have a dirnk, sorry, a drink
   Gorgon, Hydra, all the scary Wild things
You know, I think the streetlampjust went out.
Stringy hair hanging in front of her silvery eyes
Shiftsilent. Repeat after me.
Echo.
Echo.
Echo.

Andi Thomas.

Wamsutter

We had been to see an exhibition at the Baltic. The day had been sultry and somehow it had taken us an age to get there. Domain Field it was called. Jacob had snorted a great deal and become very thirsty in the process. Wiry, stainless steel, life-size figures covered the main exhibition area. We were up on the mezzanine, suspended between the ground floor and the first, overlooking the gallery.

"The metallic figures are as insubstantial as the exhibition," Jacob stated.

The figures – human in form though not content - stood, feet apart, arms dangling down at their sides, hovering by their hips.

"They look like cowboys," I said, "from 'Once Upon a Time in the West'."

I left Jacob up there and wandered down into the ghost town, for that is what it felt like, mingling amongst the metallic gunslingers. I could have been at a railroad station, walking nervously to and fro. Awaiting Charles Bronson, amongst the swelling strains of an Ennio Morricone score. The floor, unfinished cypress wood, creaking rhythmically beneath my snake boots. Suddenly Jacob jabbed me in the back, I jumped as though his index finger was a pistol. I wanted to get semi-intellectual and discuss genre typing but Jacob was plain aggressive as he strong-armed me over to the exit.

"That Gormly is a sleek little punk who thinks he's a lady killer," he said, calm as you please, once we were outside. "Jacob, if we want to talk about empty forms, then we should talk about you?"
"What do you mean by that?" he asked, fixing me one of his rare evil stares, his eyebrows puckering into some kind of self-life.
"Like when you say 'Hallelujah!' everytime something works out fine and 'Goddamn it!' when it doesn't."

Jacob took offence, striding off into silence; I, stray dog-like, followed at his heels, regretting my harsh tone, counting from one to ten in an effort to calm down, to beat the heat, to not get unhinged.

"I enjoyed the exhibition," I told myself, "it is Jacob who should be all hot under the collar."

We took the metro north to Newcastle, getting off at Gray St.
A couple in front of us were discussing a South Korean picture they were going to see at the Tyneside Cinema.

"But I warn you," the young man said, "the script not only lacks a coherent plot but even purposefully avoids the usual dramatic contrasts and development."
"That's alright by me," the young woman returned, "I've brought a jigsaw puzzle with me."
And, sure enough, under her arm, I noticed a large box. Shells of the Western Pacific in Color. 500 pieces.

At one of our regular bars, I went to the bathroom whilst Jacob got the drinks in. We discussed the exhibition a little more. Jacob labelling it as pretentious, preposterous, repellent and even media posturing. My passions were not aroused, I was not even irritated now that I was out of the heat. And this is something that is beginning to worry me a great deal: the lack of passion I seem to experience these days.

It was then that Jacob told me that the man with the crooked sunglasses, drinking rye up at the bar, claimed to be from Wamsutter.

"Well?" I queried.
"Don't you get it?" Jacob dropped his voice low, "Wamsutter is a fictional town."
"Well, we've all got to come from somewhere," I said. Jacob gave his customary snort then opened his mouth to show me his tongue was dry. A subtle hint that it was my round. "And while you are up there, ask him, why don't you."
"Ask who what?"
"The guy with the crooked sunglasses why he claims to come from a fictional town."

At the bar, I caught the barman's eye.

"Two rum and cokes, when you've got the time, Jim, oh and a rye for our friend from Wamsutter."

"Hey," the only man standing at the bar said, "I don't just let any dude buy me a drink."

"Mark," I said, extending my hand, "friend of Jacob's over there."

I jerked my free thumb back towards Jacob who shifted uneasily in his unlaced brown boots.

"I don't care for your friend, he's only friendly when things are going his way."

I noticed then that a small screw was missing from the man's sunglasses, though this was not the cause of their crookedness.

"Two rum and cokes," Jim said, slowly putting the drinks on the counter.

"Well, what about it, can I get you a rye?" I asked the man from Wamsutter.

He fixed me with overbright blue eyes, then relaxed them into something resembling a grin, "Oh, alright, Old Overholt again, Jim."

I stood at the bar, sipping my drink, smiling at our new acquaintance, forcing Jacob to come over. He picked up his drink, mumbled something about trying to find some Johnny Cash, or was it now Jonathan Richman, on the juke box and pushed off. So far the music had been all Country & Western. Grating.

"What's it like living in Wamsutter?" I asked.

"Hot, only I don't live there no more."

"Do you have any idea why my friend thinks Wamsutter is fictional?"

"Ah, the elixir of life," the man from the fictional town said, ignoring my question, lifting his rye to his lips, savouring it briefly before sipping.

"Made from a formula written on chrysanthemum leaves which grows in profusion in the area."

I lifted my rum and coke. A Girl Named Sue, or was it now Egyptian Reggae, came on the juke box.

"Wamsutter?"

"Yes, Wamsutter. If you really must know, I had to leave town on account of I stepped across the Sheriff's pillow, if you catch my drift, one hundred and seventy years ago. Fortunately I managed to bring this here elixir into exile with me," he said, scanning me with his over-intelligent eyes, evidently looking for my weak spot.

"You live here?" I asked.

"Up the coast, Whitley Bay."

"You don't sound American," I said.

"A hundred and seventy years ago not many Americans did," he retorted.

I was about to ask if Wamsutter was in the state of Texas when Jim shook his head slowly at me. I looked around and saw Jacob dancing to Egyptian Reggae, so it must have been the Jonathan Richman record after all. I went over and joined him. The man from Wamsutter looked down on the floor and spat.

Anthony Kane Evans.

The Rough Estate

A young boy says to me
I want to get out of here
I hate living here
My mates make me do bad things

A young girl says to me
Someone called me a bitch
So I scratched her car

A young boy tells me (though I haven't transcribed)
I threw a firebomb over the side
Screams
Shitting myself
Phew
Just missed the baby in a pram
Mother still crying though.

And I reply
You're still lovely inside.

Charlie Satine.

Bar

They called her Yorkie
She wasn't sweet or tasty
More a case of chunky
Thick
And incredibly popular
With long distance lorry drivers.

Jon Oyster.

Kicking Small Dogs

A confession: each small dog I see
I want to kick.

Usually I am ambivalent,
in a canine sense,

but small dogs, shoebox size,
move me.

It is not cruelty, or an urge to inflict pain,
but natural curiosity.

A long run:
arc of bootswing

meeting small dog
and soft underbelly.

I need to know how far they would fly;
it is a science:

are the houses over the road in range?
Open windows, buses, rugby posts

all cry out to be used:
apparatus of discovery.

In my dreams the dogs are silent;
the sky is always blue, cloudless,
and it is perfect.

Matt Gambrill.

:GREEN

TweedleBo!

'twas wikkid and the ravin' hordes
did slash staccato in his wake
all luvdup were the townicorns
an' Boss lads out snake

Beware the junkywhore my son
the pills that write, the laws that catch
beware the dub dub birds and shun
the furious easysnatch

He took his whistlepop in hand
long time the bangin' Bo did bust
so rested he in the chillum sea
and blissed out in it, sussed

and as in mongin' thought he sloshed
the junkywhore with veins of flame
came spazzin' through the massive mosh
a-ravin' as it came

One two One two selecta Bo!
his whistlepop went bangashrike
he hit the red and in his head
went freebase on the psyche

"and has thou sort the junkywhore?
cum to my breast, my toppish Boi
oh big up day Punani aye" -
he massive in his joy

'twas wikkid and the ravin' hordes
did slash staccato in his wake
all luvdup were the townicorns
an' Boss lads out snake

Simon Edwards.

Birch Street

Sitting on the porch outside my walk up with Elaine
watching the Friday night action on Birch Street.
Southside's so humid the air weeps.
Me and Elaine are weeping too.
Silent tears of solidarity.
She's so full of prozac she can't sleep and
I'm so drunk I can't think straight.
Her depression and my beer free our tears
from the jail we carry in our hearts.
Liberating tears hurts.
Neighbors and strangers pass by in the water vapor.
Walking in twos and fours. Driving by in souped up
cars and wrecks. Skinny, greased up gang bangers
with pants so big they sweep the street and girl friends
in dresses so tight they burn my eyes.
I can smell Miguel's Taco Stand. Hear the cool
Mexican music he plays. Sometimes I wish Elaine
were Mexican. Hot, sweet and the ruler of my passion,
but she's from North Dakota, a silent state where
you drink to feel and dance and cry.
Sailing, sailing down Birch Street. Misty boats,
street shufflers and senoritas. Off to their somewhere.
I contemplate how empty my can of beer is and
how long can I live with a woman who cries all day.
Mondays are better. I sober up and lay lines for the
Gas Company. Good clean work. Work that gives me
time to think about moving to that little town in central
Mexico I visited twenty years ago before Birch Street,
Elaine and three kids nailed my ass to this porch.

Charles P Ries.

Blinks

No one it seems is precisely sure
Where this train is going;
All that is certain
Is that it is full of people
And full of doubt.

One moment it's Manchester,
The next it's Poole
And I can't afford a coffee,
So I distract myself staring
At the sky's big blue eye.

I'm writing this in real time,
But all I want is that can of cider
That the laughing suited man opposite
Is sipping and sharing
With his worryingly sunlit girlfriend.

"I've only got one eye." My neighbour says,
"Can we swap so that I can sit by the window,
Otherwise I can't see the sea?"
"There is no sea near Manchester." I say
And the sky blinks.

David R Morgan.

LARD.

Generation gap

A magpie divebombed him
And he went home,
Got his .22,
& returned.

He shot the magpie,
Shot the nest,
Lined up all the newborn,
And he shot them too.

My father laughed
When he recounted this story.
I didn't laugh :

And years later,
A magpie divebombed me,
And I, too, went home,

But remembered that
At that time of year
Adult magpies would be protective of their newborn
& strongly defend their territories
from any potential threat.

I swore to avoid the area,
for a while,

at least
until the newborn had grown stronger enough
to leave the nest
all on their own.

Brad Evans.

The Cynical Backpacker

I climbed Sydney harbour bridge.
I saw the sun rise on Ayers Rock.
I went scuba diving on the Great Barrier Reef.
I walked through rainforests in Queensland.
I learnt to surf on the Sunshine Coast.
I went sea kayaking at Paihia.
I did the haka in Rotorua.
I saw glow worms in the caves of Waitomo.
I climbed Franz Josef glacier with an ice pick.
I played frisbee golf in Queenstown.
I rafted the rapids of Rangitikei river.
I climbed the volcano of Mt. Ngauruhoe.
I didn't jump out of a plane.
I spent the night in Auckland International.
I went mountain biking on Oahu.
I hiked the Grand Canyon in June.
I read the graffiti in gangland LA.
I walked through Harlem late at night.
I saw the joggers in Central Park.
I sketched the Niagara Falls at sunset.
I listened to the Jazz in Montreal.
I travelled thirty thousand miles.
Thirty thousand.
I need some new shoes.

Mike Cordell.

The Great Poet Sat At The Chicken Wrap Restaurant
(written at Fariba)

The great poet visits everyday
To sip coffee
To watch the world
And create a life between the fine lines of his hard-backed
companion
All time, all colours and all possibility are presented leaf after
leaf

The waitress attends to the great poet
Brings him coffee
And watches him watch the world
Imagining the life created between the fine lines of his sole
companion
Of all the time, all the colours and the possibilities leaf after
leaf

The great poet often looks toward the waitress
The waitress always looks away
He scribbles
And she wonders
Has he made a life for her?

Then one day
As she brings him cream
He says to her
"you are really cute"
she feels so disappointed

Darren Gray.

My Many, Many Brothers-In-Law

Brother-in-law No. 1

At a Christmas party, in a paper hat,
He asked me what I was good at –
I never said, but I blushed:
Standing up, with my back to the seat
Of a toilet that I have flushed,
I can tell by the refilling sound
If the toilet is blocked - before looking round.
The time between flushes is shorter;
And I know the level of the water,
Before looking round:
I can tell by the pitch of the refilling sound.
And when the water behind me is high,
I know how long it takes before
The water drops, and then I try
To flush the toilet once more.
The hat on the head of my brother-in-law –
A Christmas cracker's orange crown –
Grew grey, with wrinkled rings of brown;
Turned misty, fluffy, torn, dispersed,
As my brother-in-law was immersed
In a toilet, blocked by my shame –
My sister took his second name ...

And I, the Spiv of the Drains

My many, many brothers-in-law
Dared to go to war,
While I stayed home and spiv'd.
Some died, some lived –
                    Big deal:
There were still too many; and the real
Resistance, the real resistors
Should have been my sisters.

The cesspit spiv - the spiv of the drains:
My nephews could identify planes
Without looking up at the sky;

But they were impressed when I said that I
Could tell by the pitch of the refilling sound
If the toilet was blocked, before looking round.

Above the shish of the cistern and taps,
I heard my pregnant sister collapse
Outside the toilet door:
When the wretched name of my brother-in-law
Was no longer being cried,
I opened the door and reached outside;
And reinforced my nascent dam
By wiping myself on the telegram
I had snatched from my sister's fingers.
I left without trying to unblock it
(And maybe the water still lingers),
But before I left, I noticed a locket
On a chain, and it felt like a sign:
I had seen it used by my niece to divine
The sex of the unborn child;
She had held it over the bump, beguiled
By the promise of a baby brother;
But, one day, she would find another –
One day, my niece would want more:
She would give her brother a brother-in-law.

Thereafter, I went to the house
Of every sister whose spouse
Had been killed:
I heard them sobbing as the cisterns refilled;
And I never felt regret,
Though, once, I felt the tepid jet
Of a bidet-D-Day brother-in-law
Squirting between my crack:
A ghost-in-law, coming back
To hose me clean -
Stupidly thinking this would mean
Less paper would be needed;
But when the ghostly jet receded,
My profligacy soared:
As one hand wiped, the other one pawed
The toilet roll for my next pieces ...
I pitied the brothers of my nieces.

How many wipes could stem the torrent of a sister's love
Being switched from her brother to the groom?
Revenge is found in the smallest room.

Rogan Whitenails.

Marina Grande di Capri

Knew the moment I stepped off the boat
Sun was still baking the English potatoes
Scooters still whizzing by at 80 mph
Sea was still azure blue
For the first time the shadows had been cast on
The streets of the piazzo
Surrounded by luscious lemon trees and crispy mountains
Heads were hung low
Siesta was over, but they were sleeping
With their eyes wide open
Twitching and shaking as they dreamt of
Turbulent and choppy red seas
The lizards that once scurried around
Were now subdued
Motionless
The deafening noises, buzzing, humming, hissing
Silence

It was no longer 'che bella gurnata'
All attempts to converse were answered
With grunts and mumbles
A massacre had taken place whilst I was
Sailing
Remorse and sadness had swept the island
Like a monsoon
I felt pity
Happiness would not grow again on this
Island for a long while

Korea 2, Italy 1.

Selena Kyle.

Sunday Afternoon Sale of a Sex Manual.

She had the dull eyes
of an office worker,
the bright eyes
of an office worker on a night out.

I wanted to suggest
that a sex manual
can't change instinct
or response or spontaneity

at least not in the way that
a successful job interview can.

Neil Campbell.

it's okay there is no history
we are the pioneers
others will see the things we have built
the things we are building
and they will talk of us
in dingy pubs

Sermon Given
[Boston, Lincs.]

The sun sets inexpertly
Over these tractored fields.
But it means nothing.
Cement is cement.
Empty oil drums rattle
If you hit them with a stick.
Church is Easter. Lord

Forgive them.

A car passes a car
Going in opposite directions.
The fenland to the east
Is full of dead insects
And bad thoughts. Plunder.
Clouds coalesce. Then fray.

The words given to your lives
Are pressed flat and smell
Of cabbages. Millions of them.

Lincoln Cathedral
Northwards and yellow.
Barely surviving.

For my text. This.

A more weighted plough
Left here by accident. Olden
With a different type of God
Looking downwards. Pointing.
Monday to Friday.
Weekends as well.
Passing judgement.

Steven Taylor.

I am

The wonders of the earth such as sea sky and land
Are nothing compared to man himself
I am not impressed at all by your arguments
That proves how insignificant I am
I just know that I am
You are motivated by curiosity for the sake of it
Why concern yourself with the stars or the sky
I am not impressed by the size of the universe
This just shows how impossible I am
I just know that I am
What practical interest motivates you to think of me?
I myself am interested in my own nature
I have no interest if you need to understand my complexity
Why show me how intense I am
I just know I am

Jo Galloway.

Moonlight's Walking

Gentle greens enfold me
Entwine and riot run
Breath that moves
Now dark now light
A sigh of whispered spider's web
With drops of silver hung
The prize of moonlight's weeping
Heavy with her light
Falling now to kiss the earth
Returns to womb that gave us birth
Majestic in the night
Silent now she's walking
She's moving through the trees
Leaves whisper her passing
And call her symphony
Her eyes are beads of silver
Her skin is spider's silk
Her voice sings in branch and bough
Brought me here possessed me now
Caressed my lips and kissed my brow
Embraced me in the night
Now ever will I wander
In glades of silver-green
Each night her call I'll answer
My voice her song will sing
And when I'm old and weary
When I have served her long
She'll lay me down to rest
In gentle greens among

Wayne Miller.

Poets are interesting people

I met Jane in hospital.
Decades between us... each on a mission,
Both of us scared of losing our vision.

"They look good enough to eat", we agreed.
So we did.

I'll never forget the looks on their faces,
Patients and nurses with hands on their hips,
And the sweet taste as we munched
And consumed the whole bunch...
From the provocative vase, red,
orange
and yellow,
scrumptious.

Trish Senior.

THE YOUNG POET AND HIS PALS VISIT ... Knowlhill

In Summer 2001, Diane and me spent an amusing afternoon wandering around the hills and vales of Knowlhill, just to the west of the City.

As soon as we sat down at the top of the mysterious hill, a whole host of fairies came rushing from the trees behind us, and breezed past us on the air. For three whole minutes they came, a swarm of dancing white dots, floating away down towards the Teardrops. A few minutes later, Diane tried to roll down the hill, but found the surface too lumpy to get up much of a speed.

Knowlhill is another funny MK estate : it's not a housingy one, but rather has two halves. The east side is fields, trees and small lakes (part of the Teardrops), while the west is yet more weird faceless industry complexes. But more on those in a moment.

Whether the hill we were sat on is the Knowlhill or not, I'm not sure. Certainly from the top you can see across to the City Centre, which looks really impressive from a slight distance, many different architectural vibes clashing. I'm sorry to get so excited by looking at Milton Keynes – the greenness all around the faceless urban sprawl is much finer than the grey industrial towns I've also lived in.

At the foot of the hill are various large fields, which look like they would be fantastic for picnics and football and the like, but which probably only get used by office workers having their lunch.

We walked around the lakes, feeling a really big respect for nature, all of a sudden. Diane thought she saw a Velociraptor over the other side, but when we got there, it turned out to be sodden cardboard. We saw a heron really close up, and there were swimming birds of some ducklike sort. But I don't know what they were. It struck me that one generation ago, I would have known all of this instinctively, it seems, but now it feels like the knowledge has gone. Even my Observer Book of Wildlife is long since lost in the corners of a loft somewhere.

There were also some kind of reed / teasel things (again, y'see! I have literally no idea!), which looked peturbingly similar to a field of crucified hamsters. Go and look. You'll see what I mean...

A brief sojourn across some stepping stones, and the climb of the hill later, and we discovered a secret path. Unlike many of the paths in MK, it seemed to be a forbidden path of mystery, climbing into a green-lined tunnel almost, and winding around to a destination unknown. Except then we discovered it led back to the top of the hill again. D'oh!

Having sated our quest for knowledge amidst the wond'rous bounds of nature (and having giggled uncontrollably at the big daisies we saw), we took a stroll down what seemed to be the main industry road. It often beats me as to what all these office complexes are for, even the brand names seem mysterious on some of them. In Knowlhill it's no different, although at least many of the buildings have windows here.

One large glass-orientated collection of blocks had the name "Consumer Research and Testing Centre" (or something like that), so we decided to go inside. There was a big publicity display in the foyer past the revolving door, but after a cursory glance, the fear came upon us all a-sudden, and we had to leave.

Down at the end of the road, we finally found what we'd been searching for : the industry estate burger van. They've all got 'em, some more than one. This van had deckchairs to sit in while you waited. It doesn't get much better than this, we decided, reclining while our burgers cooked.

So, north of the Bowl, south west of the city : Knowlhill. It sums up neatly (very neatly if you're writing an article on it) both the partially accurate running joke about Milton Keynes (faceless shining industry hive) ; and also the often forgotten truth (green explorable expanses of random wildlife among the industry).

Meanwhile, the middle managers sit alone at their desks. And in Conniburrow, Gino turns up every day without fail. Even though it's hot, and the inside of the kebab van starts to drip with condensation. Even though his clientele are mainly pissheads and mouthy children. He's always there. And he always provides the meat we need to live. I'd rather he was on my side than the middle managers. I think.

Boat Story

the waterways seduce them –
canal desire.
they find themselves a boat and
spend nights of narrow love
nosing like otters.
he grows whiskers and a taste for fish,
she swirls and contorts in the water,
every slippery, acrobatic act
a feat of mind over muscle.

there is something Victorian about them –
urchins, riverside rats.
they're tinted in shoreline squalor
by the thick brown canals
and the sepia sunlight
up to their mucky mitts in mud and algae.
while Bourneville is busy mixing chocolate,
they play and preen,
lick each other clean
and love each other out the dry.

they are gluttons for nourishment
and an affront to public health.
their boat is a lair of
bones and scales and eyes and idleness;
the floor a silky riddle of
guts and fluids.
it reeks.
it creaks of tyres on the concrete quay.
it stinks of too much pleasure
for a pleasureboat moored so close
to such a mess of tarmac,
the visceral twists of merging motorways.

but the tailbacks and catastrophe
just happen around them.
city otters simply float on their backs
and relax. sometimes,
if you close your eyes,

heavy traffic can sound like the sea.

Cissy Aeon.

Only Change.

There is no death;
Only Change.
What was once a star
Is now a creature.
And when that creature is no more
T'will become a rock
Or some other feature.

Simon Chambers.

A Gathering of Fugitives
[for Peter Porter]

I

There are lice in Santa Claus' beard,
He is wearing black jack boots proofed
Against fall-out, his sledge is gilded
With swastikas, pulled by Jewish deer.
He will die of exposure on rooftops,
His going mourned in plastic churches
And tears will be specially sent from Rome.

II

I cannot remember the fate of Jack
On his beanstalk; perhaps the insecticide
Blistered his hands and they fell off.
A folk etymologist should preserve the story,
Proving that the stalk itself was phallic,
The giant's club an especially large member,
Jack's climb a retreat from mother.

III

The poet dare not discuss himself,
Instead slinks round the 'objective world'
Of his peers, observing that it only seems
To exist, that he is hovering like a fly
Round the specious grin of 'the real',
That 'deep inside him' vacancy hangs
Like dust on an airless day.

Barry Tebb.

129

Nikki Ibbotson

the Artist

Don't copy nature too literally, art is abstraction;
draw art as you dream in nature's presence,
and think more about the act of creation than about the final
result. - Gauguin

In second-hand light
He is watching the grey fluid eddy between
Green yellow enamel and a crumpled heap of
Living flesh and hair.
It   is uneven.

The Artist knows that if he could capture this moment -
As the morning blindly runs its fingers through the furrows
Of the night before,
He would have achieved something more.

More than depictions of the impassioned throes
Of fantastic life
Remastered.
More than the perfect curve of her neck.

And he would breath deeply,   it   would be complete.

Tom Chapman.

Lost

answers to the name of Gail,
black lab cross, white bib and tail
sunglasses (retro)
(frames in red)
Braun electric toothbrush head
Eels cd proof of ID,
copy of KERRANG! (unread)

house keys, car keys,
black rucksack
"The Hitch Hikers Guide..."
(in paperback)
train ticket, plane ticket
Bostick glue
lighter (underwear)
rhapsody in blue

MY LEFT SHOE
(and they were new!)
if found
please reply
(very soon)

...thank you!

Lucy Van Pelt.

A Childish Snap

the impatient posed
photograph
of me age six,
a look down
betrays my love
of dandelions
and beetles,
thirty eight
years later,
it still does.

John G Hall.

'council pay glow'

lying in cushions of plucked flight,
twelve years old and full of holes,
i stir up the pages with my mind's eyelight,
til they're damped away by somniacs' growls.
the streetlamp hum looks like diluted blood
on the smeary windowglass, or baby's milk
and grenadine, bleaching the glittery buds
an accident orange beside the night noises' lilt.

Rachel George.

evolution, Evolution, EVOLUTION

I'm the pinnacle
of over
two thousand years
of evolution

All defects
have been
slowly removed
over time

I'll live
to at least eighty

I'm smarter
faster
stronger
and more handsome
than my great
great
great
great
grandfather
who by the way
died at forty

I stand
at the very brink of space
the whole universe
in the palm
of my hand
bound by nothing
not nature
not science

not even god

I am a god

Now
where'd i leave
my shoes?

Paul Grant.

please now take these mirrors away
from me, all i can see are
just more mirrors, please

tell me that you will not change me
oh please tell me
the city changes me

rain poem

I rain within myself
Catching the drops as they fall
Hoping for a beam of light
To make a rainbow

Rachel Dillon.

Diving

I'm trying to persuade you to go underwater,
to put you into worlds I wouldn't dare to visit.
You dream of slicing the heads of snakes and ask about sharks.
I insist it's perfectly safe, you complain the fish stare at you
insolently,
making you feel you're not welcome there.
Invisible stinging creatures turn your skin red and itchy.
I brush aside my own fears of drowning,
sucking water into the lungs,
the stars in the river and jumping for air.
Only in my sleep can I still save her,
and even there it seeps into me,
the knowledge that it's too late,
like something I have always known, but has sunk to the bottom,
the ship wreck of her dying.

Aoife Mannix.

Pluto

It was minus 4 outside. Enough to tell you to stay inside. But then, on the news, on the radio, they said it was minus 54 in Finland. I thought of them then, the Finns, with their winter wheels on but that wouldn't do them much good now, they wouldn't even be able to go outdoors. They said, on the radio, that it was so cold in Finland that the Finns themselves couldn't even listen to the radio.

"Just think," I said to my girlfriend, *"they might not even know that it's minus 54 themselves."*
"Who?" Jackie asked, not paying much attention.
"The Finns, that's who."
"Who cares what the Finns think!"

I went out. I wasn't exactly in a good mood, me and the girlfriend were having a bit of an argument about where to place the new cupboard we'd just got. I'd spent all afternoon assembling the damn thing then suddenly she wanted to put it where the sofa was.
"And just where's the telly going to go?" I'd said.

I didn't have the energy to go into the town, or maybe it was the cold that kept me on the estate, anyway I just went over to *The Cat & The Pigeon* and bought myself a *Murphy's*, which was their last month's 'Pint of the Month'

"What happened to the Old Horizontal?*"* I shouted at Joe, the landlord.
That was supposed to be this month's pint.
"Bloody weather, couldn't get it through, could they?"

There were no free tables and it was overcrowded at the bar, so I sat down next to the Greenlander. He'd arrived on the estate about a year back. Nobody knew what he did until Jimmy saw him outside Tesco's washing the windows a month or so back.
"So, what's he doing," I'd asked Jimmy, *"working for Tesco's or cleaning windows?"*
"He's a window cleaner isn't he, good business if you've got

the right connections."
It turned out that the Greenlander, who nobody had ever talked to as far as I could gather, had bought Bob's old round.

Brian was in the pub, shooting pool with some of the lads but I was pissed off with him, somebody had seen him hit Eileen, his wife, outside the butcher's it'd been. So, I sat down next to the Greenlander.
"I hear you bought Bob's old round?"
He looked up at me, the brown eyes a little glazed.
"Bob, the one who lost his leg in that freak accident?" I elaborated.
"Bob ... freak ... yeah."

He smoked his cigarettes, I read The Mirror. There was a lot to complain about, in the paper I mean, but I couldn't get the Greenlander interested in anything.
"Thinking of disqualifying Pluto they are," I said.
"Pluto?" the Greenlander suddenly seemed to wake up a bit.
"Yeah, the planet, you know, them astronauts don't think it's a real planet, 500 hundred of them are going to vote on its status, it says here. Odds are it'll be knocked down to an asteroid."
There was a potted history of the planet Pluto.

"It says here that it's only a clump of ice! Discovered in Arizona it was, back in the thirties, imagine discovering a clump of flying ice in the hot deserts of Arizona."
"Pluto has always been a pariah in the game of the planets, said Bjorn Frank Jorgensen, director of ... some observatory or other."
The Greenlander went to the bar and came back with two pints of *Murphy's*.
"Cheers!" I said, somewhat surprised, as he set one before me.
"The bear man is wrong," the Greenlander said, swaying slightly.
I didn't know what he was talking about but I reckoned he must've started drinking some time in the afternoon. Probably too cold to be window-cleaning on a day like this. I decided to stick to the text. *"It says here that the 500 astronauts ..."*
"Astronomers," he corrected looking over my shoulder, down at the paper.
"Yeah, well, they reckon an ice clump can't be a planet."

141

"Why not, Saturn's only made up of gas."
He re-seated himself.
"Is it really?" I asked across the table.
He didn't volunteer any further information so I continued:
"Well, somebody in this magazine, Science they call it, reckons Pluto should be regarded as a trans-Neptune object, seems that they've discovered another, smaller clump of ice somewhere at the back of Neptune."
"Next they'll be disqualifying continents," the Greenlander said.
"And countries," I put in, *"Like Iceland!"*
"Iceland is green, Greenland is ice," he said.
"Go on, you're kidding?"
The Greenlander shook his head.
"Are you serious?"

But he wasn't really listening, he just carried on shaking his head. He began mumbling something low, it rumbled out of him slowly, like a chant or a dark poem.

The jagged mountain peaks,
like gleaming sword-blades against an absinthe green sky.
After the storm comes the fog, grey and ghostly.
Deadening every sound it settles soft and thick and heavy on sea and ice.
But lifting, the fog is tinged with light from the sky above.
Blurred outlines emerge like threatening shadows.
A puff of wind and she is there.

I went back to my newspaper. When I got to the sports section I found out that City had lost, I'd forgotten they'd played mid-week, they were still dangling on the outskirts of the qualification box but had lost a bit of ground whereas I'd had hopes they'd climb into it. It put a bit of a downer on me that piece of news did, still I bought the next round, setting the Greenlander's pint down, carefully, in front of him. He was still shaking his head, fractionally.

When I got home Jackie had gone and moved the cupboard herself.
"We hadn't agreed to put it there," I said.
"As soon as you set foot in the pub we did," she replied, always

quick. I made a pot of tea, I didn't want us to go to bed sulking. When I opened the fridge for the milk I noticed that the icebox was just about frozen over, a stalactite was beginning to stretch down to the top shelf, threatening to impale the cheddar. It made me think about Pluto and the Greenlander and his strange poem.

"Did you know that Greenland was just a clump of ice?" I called out.
"Who've you been drinking with, Jimmy?" Jackie shouted back.
"No, no ... it was just something I read in the paper," I said, grabbing the milk and firmly shutting the fridge door.

Anthony Kane Evans.

Night Life

Have you ever seen
a MK sunset after rain,
when steel and glass shimmers
reflecting snakes of red taillights
heading homewards towards
Emerson Valley or Springfield,
with drivers shielding their eyes from
a low sun as it finally dips behind
the flat roofs of Fullers Slade when
the neon lights of George's Fish Bar
flicker into life as the night begins.

David Gildner.

Haiku for Someone

when was the last verse
that anyone ever sent
to you in Haiku?

it's not so easy
you must count the syllables
and have some meaning

this line must be 5
and this one must be 7
and make you feel whole

do you feel at ease
at having read this poem?
or are you dismayed

confused and sad man
seeking sensitive woman
to help counting words

Andy Pearson.

Le lac de ma coeur

Up high,
in that mountain pass,
framed
by that alpine grass,
where those peaks
begin to break,
there it lies,
that beautiful lake.
And sometimes girls
will stop to admire,
its waters shimmer
with that golden fire.
Maybe they'll smile
and go for a paddle,
down by the bank,
where the waters babble.
But do they ever
stop to wonder,
or pause for thought,
before they dive under?
Maybe they don't care
at the river,
if you're a paddler,
or really a swimmer.
But does it nece-
-ssarily follow,
that this lake
should be just as hollow?

Mike Cordell.

DAVE'S COMET

Steve Groom.

:PINK

Pigeons

'I hate fucking pigeons',
the girl outside Euston station said to her friend
as they scattered fries
and pigeon wings

I had just been to a conference
On 'Linguistic Context
and Interpretation'
which got me thinking about what it was
she hated so much.
Was it the pigeons? Or the act of congress,
beak and feather?

Why do you do it then, I thought, and asked her;
'Why do you do it then?'

She looked at her friend,
fry-handed,
and then at me.

'What did you say?'

And so I told her, again.

'Fuck off', she said, and walked away,
muttering.
'Weirdo!' her friend shouted back,
while I stared at the pigeons
and the fries
and the dirt.

Matt Gambrill.

the mink & the fox

there was once a pink mink
who, during the dark days of December,
plucked her eyebrows,
packed her Polaroid,
filled a hip-flask with fish-flavoured vodka
and headed North to the great white wastes,
to the thinner and more lucid air
where all there is is seamless snow and the hush of potential
and where there is always a mythical silence to the weather.

in a remote forest along the way, she met a blue fox. they
spent a silent few hours circling each other, admiring each
other's coats and eyeing each other up, until finally the fox
felt satisfied and safe enough to sit still in strange company.
so the mink demurred and joined him. she brought out her
vodka and the fox shared a suck or two on his harmonica and
all was deliciously cordial. the late afternoon turned to evening
turned to night, and by the time the stars had begun their slow,
exhausting trawl across the sky, cordiality turned to familiarity
turned to flirtation.

"listen"
said the fox, licking his lips of fishy liquor,
"my dear mink, we are so very much alike. we are both on the
run. we are both young, healthy, well-groomed and have
sparkling teeth. we are of one mind. we're one of a kind."

"i agree"
purred the mink and raised one vaulted eyebrow.
"do go on."

"we are so beautiful, you and i, that we can do anything"
added the fox,
"and you have such a lovely and well-tailored pelt of pink that
i am sure you have a silken lining on the inside..."

giggled the mink,
"what *can* you mean?"
and winked one heavy eyelid like a fan of ostrich feathers. she

151

took out her Polaroid and gave it to the fox.
"here"
she whispered,
"take my picture."

and so, in the blink of her made-up eyes, they were soon
snapping at each other and littering the white woodland floor
with a cartoon strip of dancing, laughing, playing the harmonica
and sharing little midnight snacks of mice and voles; of the
mink blowing kisses and the fox frowning darkly. both bristled
from the follicles up and they soon became too hot for their
thick coats. so they unzipped each other and slipped themselves
shod, peeling off slowly and posing for each other in their
smooth and tender underneathnesses. before they knew it they
had made love one two three four five *six* times, pausing
inbetween for mutual photo sessions. the night slicked by in
a salacious fable of fluids, of fur, of musk glands and
masturbation, of teeth, teats and tingling skin. and when the
vodka was spent, the fox tucked away his bulbous white tail
and the mink lit up a rollie.

"i'm heading North"
she said,
"to the great white wastes, to the thinner and more lucid air
where all there is is seamless snow and the hush of potential
and where there is always a mythical silence to the weather...
want to come?"

the fox kissed one of her six full teats and said,
"i thought you'd never ask."

so, with the sunrise just about to make its first faux-pas, it was
beneath the pink blush of a morning sky that the mink giggled,
got dressed and linked fates with the fox.

they decided to catch a train
and charmed themselves aboard a wasteward express flashing
false passports and smiles. the fox tipped his hat to strangers
and played poker with the passengers, while the mink accepted
flatteries and fawn-coloured compliments.

outside, through the carriage windows, the countryside shivered

fast and white with shutter-speed and snow; great glossy tracts
of unmanageable land were rendered two-dimensional, like
scenery set for a pantomime or morality-play; while inside,
shapely conspiracies formed themselves between the crushed
velvet upholstery and the hushed, smoked glass.

"The fox is too louche"
they said,
*"too in love with himself and too tongue-smooth for
our liking. No doubt he has a garotte coiled inside
his smokey jacket, or else a pen that propels poisoned ink!"*

and:

*"Look at the mink in her curvy fur collar and creamy
lip-gloss! So sure of herself and so snap-happy, so
clinically clickety-click with those cagey eyelashes of
hers - a cabaret vamp for sure, a spy maybe. They're
not to be trusted!"*

the mink then found herself sitting amidst a miasma of question-
marks. she watched a sickly chocolate-box of landscapes sugar
by, complete with wild woods and fairytale dustings of snow,
but she couldn't help feeling that burning dark and bitter
underneath were currents of concentrated, volatile liquid, the
ulterior centres of liqueurs or Molotov cocktails.
she did not feel entirely safe.

she checked her mascara in a flurry of self-consciousness. it
occurred to her that events were conspiring – and that there
were five possible plots afoot:

1) this could be a tale of love,
of unzipped vulnerabilities and of saving each other's skin.
there'd be plenty of sepia flashbacks and misty-eyed dulcimer
sounds from the mink's tragic past or the fox's muddy origins.
 all very poignant and widescreen.

2) this could be a tale of betrayal,
of telephone wires tapped and extra-marital beds bugged,
smeared decoy scents and spanner sabotage. it could involve
blackmail: black-&-white Polaroids in manila envelopes or sexual

trickery at the very most tenuous edges of the civilised world, and all for the ambiguous abstractions of Politics or Faith.

3) maybe a tale of clashing vanities:
cruelty, disfigurement, covetousness –
broken shards of mirror used to cut and scar and shred and mar and leave the shivering, ugly little insides to suffer from exposure.

4) a tale of cloaked identity,
where they would soon discover that they were proven – by paper, by blood and by those double helices of history (the twists of Fate and DNA) – to be brother and sister, and where the collusions of the gene-pool would mean the mink gave birth to a mutated litter of six, a purple mix: a fink, a minx, a fix, a mix & two rather raggedy mox.

or finally,

5) this could be a tale of epiphany,
of mystical catharsis in the wilderness, of rapture and a shedding of earthly skins, catching transcendence like hypothermia.

she snapped her mirror shut.
a terrible prescience was pressing down on her. she had struggled hard to disentangle herself from all that fable-nóir, but was somehow still pursued by the cumbersome mechanics of Fate, which had moved heaven and earth to make a moral point, to make an example of her. and even as she and the fox hurtled toward the wonder hinterlands, she could begin to smell, like ozone, the territorial smears of border-checks and surveillance cameras. Paranoia rifled through her carpetbag and rummaged in the pockets of her fur. it found microdots, cyanide capsules, a revolver, grenades and the fox's secret dossier...

oh, duplicitous mink!
traitorous mink!
scheming and immoral mink!
... well, naturally she had none of these. but Fate would find *something* on her person, had maybe already planted it. she could well imagine the diabolical telltales that were being

developed in some dark room in the city even now, and almost wished she'd stayed safe on the farm. the prospect of being allowed to get away and live in uncomplicated amorality with her dashing fox was becoming as remote as their intended destination, even as they sped closer to it.

it was after many card games and gulps of vole-flavoured vodka that she finally put this predicament to the fox. he had the answer instantly, as if he'd been waiting for her to ask but though she'd never do so.

"it's simple"
he said,
"we are only bound by our hides. we must divest ourselves of our disguises, for they are what implicate us in this plot. let's leave behind vain and anthropomorphic conceit. let some other wolf in sheep's clothing make an ass or a scapegoat of themselves. we can slip the trap if we just undress. are you with me?"

and so,
from that point on they renounced the power of speech,
and as soon as they arrived at the blankness of the sleek, bleak tundra, they shrugged off their mortal coats and froze flat into a picturebook tableau,
bare, uncensored and entirely apocryphal.

untraceable by footprints or rhetoric, scandal or dental records, they vanished very quickly and very ever after, leaving only a trail of obscene photographs in their wake,
and no sign of a moral whatsoever.

Cissy Aeon.

Trolley Song

Fuck you and the concrete cow
you rode in on
On the grassy slope
by the Peace Pagoda
I sit with bourbon
stinging in my throat
and ripping up your letters
one by one

The sun is slowly rising
And my battered army greatcoat
wet with dew
(I have had this coat since
before you and I will have it
after too)

The redways slick with slugs
The city opens up its arms
to welcome me back

And two weeks later
I am pushed in a trolley
home from Bar Central
by a skinny boy
two years younger than me

You never liked the houses
in Downhead Park (soulless you said)
And sometimes I agreed
But now -

With his hands behind my neck
With his lips upon my face
The houses are cheering
All the windows light up
and I realise just how wrong you were.

Kate Silver.

his girl goldfish muse

he asked me to have his child
he smiled
and explained he'd always wanted one
he would raise it on his own
said he'd had enough practise
at being alone
insisted that it wouldn't cost me a penny
he'd rob a bank to get money
before they disconnected his phone.
we decided that it would be beautiful
pretty like him/me
we would take it away
go stay in Cuba
(start revolution
at the age of 3)
and this child would be really special
we'd water it well
and watch it grow
but eventually i found out
the reason he'd asked me
only because kirsty had said no.

Lucy Van Pelt.

The monkeys on the roof

Every morning I am woken up by the monkeys on the roof
They go **"Whoo, hoo-hoo, whoo, hoo-hoo"**
My wife says **"They're not monkeys! They're just birds"**
But I know they're monkeys
They live on the roofs of all the houses in our street
And they go **"Whoo, hoo-hoo, whoo, hoo-hoo"**
In the mornings just to wake us up

They make the monkeys in the house dance
You know, the ones who live in the cupboards
In the spaces beneath the bed, under the stairs
In the wardrobes and in the drawers
These monkeys don't go **"Whoo, hoo-hoo"**
They just dance – silently
Waving their long arms

The monkeys on the roof are small
They're all little greyish-brown monkeys
Like you see on the telly
The ones in the house are actually apes
But I call them monkeys, because it sounds cute
Not to their faces, obviously, they might be offended
They're very small as well, but bigger than the roofmonkeys

Sometimes my wife looks at me strangely
She says **"There are no monkeys!"**
And expects me to believe her!
As if! There are monkeys everywhere
Everyone knows that!
They just don't come out and dance for just anyone
They're very shy and very, very small

When I tell people about the monkeys
They look at me strangely
As if there was something wrong with me
But I know they've seen and heard them too
You can tell these things
Everybody loves monkeys as much as I do
They just don't all admit to it

When I told my wife she looked like a monkey
She didn't take it as a compliment
She went all shouty and made a bad face
That made her look even more like a monkey
When I told her this she went away
There's no work anymore, but I still get up early
And call out "Whoo, hoo-hoo" to all my little friends

Paul Rafferty.

To Elle

Hey you
You still smoking?
Did you ever learn to drive?
Are your pages all still full?
Are your eyes still wide and open like satellite
    dishes?
Did you ever eat a monkey?
Ever find out where chewing gum comes from?
Do you still kick your left leg when you sleep?
Do you still have the same secrets or have you
    told a few?
Did you ever find someone who could talk more than
    once an hour?
I never did work out
What speed
You were meant to be played at
Was it 33 or 45?
With hindsight
I think it was 78
Do you still dream of horses?
Did you ever?
Do you still have 36 eyelashes on your left eye
And 38 on your right?
Do you still taste of static?
Does your smile still look like someone else's?
As if you bought it
From a second hand clothes shop
But it doesn't quite fit
Is your youth still sonic neon?
Or has your bulb dimmed a little?
Do you still get so drunk
That you fall over and put cuts across your back?
Are you still felt-tipped and electric?
Do you still smell of fresh paint?
Do you remember the time
The heel of your shoe
Broke off
And I played hero
And found it?

In your absence
I do.

Paul Grant.

163

THE YOUNG POET REMEMBERS ... BAR CENTRAL

MK's best ever provider of Indie Nights finally closed its doors in 2004 - and in a break from visiting estates, we chose to remember it with this epitaph.

Strangely, I am writing this on a Saturday morning, without a hangover. It clearly wasn't a Bar Central night last night...

When I wanted to go out and dance to music I liked; and when I wanted to go out and try and find pretty people to dance with; and when I wanted to see good local bands play live; and when I just needed a night out, there was only one place to go in Milton Keynes, and that was Bar Central.

Now sadly closed forever after years of providing us with our only real place to hear alternative music, I thought it only fitting I should raise this glass, this final double-vodka-and-coke, to the place where we dreamed a thousand dreams, slurred a thousand speeches, and stumbled around the dancefloor to a thousand Indie hits.

BC wasn't the greatest nightclub in the world, but it was ours. I will be the first to admit that I didn't go there so much anymore, as my twenties waned I started to feel a bit too much like a dodgy old man for comfort, but knowing it was there was enough for me. Now, there is nothing. Perhaps it's fitting that the doors should close for the final time just a week or two before the death of John Peel. Like the Great Man himself, I thought Bar Central would be around for ever, and like the Great Man also, a big part of my teens and twenties has disappeared, possibly never to be replaced.

My memories of Bar Central are so many, so blurred, so emotional, so hazy. I have been there to try and pull (only very occasionally did I succeed) ; I have been there to see bands (and a couple of times to play ourselves!) ; more often than not, I have been there just to hear songs I liked. Where else in Milton Keynes am I ever going to hear "Come Out 2Nite" by Kenickie being played, other than my own bedroom?

164

My memories include (and every tribute is a personal one, obviously – Bar Central was many things to many people!): Neil always standing at the door with the bouncers, or behind the bar, hectic ; me and James doing a kind of Jarvis Cocker showdown to "Common People" in the middle of the dancefloor while the nu-metal kids looked on, bemused ; Underhill's short-lived Sunday Jazz Nights, where we attempted to sell Monkey Kettle by sitting in a corner hoping someone would ask us what it was ; always meeting someone you used to know, or know vaguely, and usually for me also my little brother being there smashed off his box ; me and Maj smashing a table by accident and being asked to leave ; the horrible toilets ; the short-lived experiment of selling chips ; trying to chat up the pretty door-girl with the appalling gambit "Excuse me, I've just been bitten by a man in your nightclub. Is that my fault, or the nightclub's fault?" ; teenagers practising their Jackass wrestling moves in the corner...

So many Bar Central songs, for better or worse : "One Step Closer" (Linkin Park) ; "BBC" (from Austin Powers) ; "Debaser" (The Pixies) ; "I Would Fix You" (Kenix) ; "Pure Morning" (Placebo) ; "No One Knows" (QOTSA) ; "Common People" (Pulp) ; "Trouble" (Shampoo) ; even "Killing In The Name" (RATM). And I always have a soft spot for the reaction which Helen and Diane gave to the 5ive "Hits Medley". Or maybe you had to be there. I was.

Perhaps I'm not just sad about BC, perhaps it's a kind of general sadness about the ending of what feels like one chapter of my life. Certainly it had its flaws, I'm sure when I took my friends who live in London there they seemed relatively underwhelmed, but that's not the point. Our lives happened there for some time, It Was Where We Went.

I don't know where I'll go for an Indie Night Out now, I don't know if anywhere will replace it successfully. I already hear rumours about possible alternatives, and I'm sure we'll give them a go. But maybe something has changed in me also. Although looking at my Daredevil digital wristwatch, my dyed black hair and my desire to buy the Help She Can't Swim album on the way home, perhaps not so much has changed after all.

Perfect Stranger

She sits diagonally opposite me
Swaying gently with the movement of the train.

Her perfectly sculpted face is composed and still,
Slim face supporting narrower nose,
Precise in its beauty.

Dyed black hair frames her face,
Fair roots beginning to show through
As the tips fade to chestnut.

Delicate freckles pattern her nose and cheeks;
A faint dusting of powder highlights her eyelids;

Carefully coloured lips gently part in sleep,
Moistened occasionally by a lazy tongue.

Eyelids quiver as she thinks or dreams.
Head slowly nodding forward as sleep takes hold.

She stirs and wakes
Showing clear blue eyes
And grants me a smile.

Rachel Dillon.

I sent you a scorpion

I was thinking of a flower
>> But flowers go bad
> old + wilting.

When outside the boulangerie
>> Near to where a sweet little
>>> dog stood

I found you this.
>> I thought it would travel better.
I don't. I waited at half a dozen
>>> Aires just today
>> And yesterday.

We went all the way from page 124 to p.2.
> And now it's ours, in a special box, called Cirrus ;
and with a claw broken.

Bunny.

Kaz-Org The Golem Attempts (Badly) To Explain To His New Girlfriend Why He's Fifty Five Minutes Late For Their Romantic Meal At the Thai Bistro.

"I'M CONCRETE AND I'M CRUEL.
GOT GREAT GREY HANDS, GOT TARMAC SKIN, AND DIRTY."

"I've been waiting since eight thirty!"

"BUT I AM WASTELAND, I AM GRANITE -
THE VEINS THAT CHOKE THIS ROTTING PLANET!"

"The bistro can't be full up, can it?
The reservation's not till ten o'clock..."

"I AM THE MIGHTY AGE-OLD LORD OF ROCK!
MY MUSCLES GRRRIND, AND GRAVEL IS MY SWEAT!!"

"You weren't like this on Friday, when you met
Samantha and my friends from work!"

"I THUNDER AND I RAGE : BESERK!!
MY STAGE; A CHURNING MASS - TECTONIC POWER!!!"

"I can't believe you let me stand here, freezing, for an hour!"

"THIS INSOLENCE MUST CEASE! I AM THE SLATE-STERN REAPER!
THE SHOVELLER OF DARKLIT CAVES AND DEEPER!!"

"My mother's right, I should have married Dieter.
He's rational and forthright, always civil in his tone.
He works in merchant banking and he isn't made of stone.
And some might say his wage puts him above you!"

(she turns to leave)

"BUT CYNTHIA... I LOVE YOU!!!"

matthew michael taylor.

I Hum On Trains

I hum on trains because I can,
mmm.
No-one knows if it's me or the engine,
mmm.

Alpot Strobe.

the Power Of television On the Psyche Of My Friend Frank

I came through into the living room. Frank was shaking like a leaf, pressing the on/off button on the remote over and over again.

"What is it?", I asked.
"Me", he said.

The television kept flickering on and then off in tune with Frank's thumb movements. I prised the remote from his firm grasp. Clicked definitively off.

"<u>Frank!</u>"

I felt like I should slap him across the face, bring him back to himself. However, I restrained myself. I was the host, he my guest. I was bringing through a bottle of 'inferior' red wine to go with the classic Monte Hellman picture I had picked up cheap on video.

"What is it, Frank?"
"<u>Me.</u>"

His eyes met mine.
"I ... I was in a short film, just now, on the television. In a disco, I was, insulting some guy about his age."

"Well, it couldn't have been you, could it", I said, absurdly putting reassurance into the tone.
"No," he replied, *"<u>absolutely not</u>; and yet, yes, it was me!"*

The telephone rang. It was Jacob.

"I've just seen Frank in a bad short. You didn't tell me he was doing any acting."
"Well, he's not, not as far as I know", I replied.
"It wasn't me", Frank called out, almost in tears, *"and yet ... it was."*

When my girlfriend, Rebecca, came over, she was angry with me.
"You never told me that Frank was an actor."
"He's not!" I protested.

"And yet, curiously, I find I am", Frank said.
"Oh, hi Frank, didn't see you over there in the corner and all."

He had drank almost all the red. An Italian. *Biferno.*

"You were good", Rebecca said, *"on the telly, I mean."*
"It wasn't him!" I shouted.
"No, it's alright", Frank said, *"I'm getting used to the idea."*

Anthony Kane Evans.

Angel

There's a cold empty space in my bed tonight,
My far off dreaming.
Filled only by the letter you wrote.
You made my curtains fit,
And filled the air with you,
And I can't stop smiling.
There's a cold empty space in my bed tonight,
My far off dreaming.
reminded of Trains and Thai chicken,
And trips to the mud.
Always smiling.
There's a cold empty space in my bed tonight,
My far off dreaming.
Hold me till the morning and then some more.
Kissing, smiling, loving.
There's a cold empty space in my bed tonight,
My far off dreaming.
Come back soon.

Steven M Kendall.

Canal
Fenny
Stratford

Chrissie Williamson.
174

e-motion, e-mail

he spun a tale that crackled and sparked,
words meant to inspire,
a mousey click, dispatched it quick,
'cross yards of copper wire.

she chose her options, selected fonts,
as best as she was able,
a response so chaste, returned with haste,
through lengths of shielded cable.

he liked her style, revealed his thoughts,
lines that she could share,
remotely penned, he still could send,
vibrating waves of air.

she tapped her keys, and thought and smiled,
ideas sprang up and ran,
were sent to screen, in blue and green,
across the corporate LAN.

one day he let a thought run loose,
a heartfelt fleeting notion,
but worded jewels, hit system rules,
suppressing all emotion.

she saw some sunlight through the trees,
emotional and clever,
although she mailed, the system failed,
and lost her thoughts forever.

his worried fingers keyed once more,
supposedly protected,
but the file prepared, became ensnared,
- a virus had infected.

she lost all hope, she turned away,
all remnants duly trashed,
a file abending, a sad, small ending,
the relationship had crashed.

Andy Pearson.

Caved In

Crazy Coco's in Cardiff
Was more a coal pit
Than a nightclub.
Full of minors,
Wall to wall coke,
Well stacked slag
In the corner.
You just took your pick
And went home
With something off it's face.

Jon Oyster.

Well, phone Mike. Maybe he's seen it. Ok.

Hi, yeah, Mike?
Hi Mike, right listen,
have you seen the remote?
Yeah, someone moved it.
what? No, I checked there,
yeah, and there.
Well, if it was I wouldn't be ringing you would I?
Jesus.
Well, can you remember where you last had it?
Right, right, right, well what were you doing with it in there?
Oh I see... fair enough, I'll check it out.
Cheers man seeya later.
click.
Did he know?
Apparently he thinks he might have left it in the bathroom.
*Oh........................ what was he doing with it in the
bathroom?*

Simon Edwards.

The Letter

I lied
When I said
That I enjoyed very much
The letter you sent me

In truth
I was so busy
Pressing the parts
That you might have licked
All over my body
That
I forgot
To read
The words
You wrote.

Paul Grant.

Maggie Cheung

The cats in her neighbourhood
do not want the actress, Maggie Cheung,
to reprise her role as Irma Vep,
the latex-suited, sleek cat-burgling vamp.

When she took the part,
Maggie Cheung decided to steal eight lives from every cat
and found, to her immense relief,
she was naturally able to play the part
of the light fingered thief.

Maggie Cheung has now promised only the black cat
will get its eight lives back
if it gives her enough luck
to land her an Oscar within the year.

So now, whenever Maggie Cheung walks down the street,
the black cat walks in front of her
and crosses her path a dozen times

to make sure
the good luck
is sewn up
and cannot come undone.

Thomas McColl.

Moon Lee

You like to play around with death.
You make it look cute.
You dress it up in a short skirt,
a panda sweater,
and a cute hat with a bobble on top.

To you, death is light, cheap and fizzy like candy pop.
You are a killing machine.
When death cries out for more
You place a blood-soaked dummy in its mouth.

You are thirty six,
but look as young as you did at sweet sixteen.
It is said you never age,
for death itself is afraid to meet you.

Moon Lee,
you are invincible.
Even on that inevitable day
when you find yourself at death's door,
you'll be asking if it wants to come out and play.

Thomas McColl.

Boy Loses Girl

Boy meets girl.
Boy loses girl.
Boy wishes he had bought
A lost key detector,
Attached it to girl,
Then he could whistle,
And girl would beep
When boy was nearby.
Girl, however, is resourceful,
Goes to tourist information centre,
Catches the number 63 bus.
On the way home,
Girl meets new boy.
Boy now spends every six months
Whistling outside girl's toilets
Waiting for a beep.

Selena Kyle.

That Glorious Pulp

Buster Cooper
With a pile of comics half as tall as us.
His parents were loaded.
Rich-coloured sagas he had of *The Flash* and *Superman*,
Black and white books about Texas Rangers,
Medieval stuff in *Classics Illustrated*.
We swapped a few, but looking at that thick wad he
Walked off with my mouth watered.

Years later he came round with an even bigger load
When he was WORKIN'.
I was into Rider Haggard and H.G.Wells
And didn't have a *Batman* or a *House of Mystery* to my name.

Then one day I was afflicted with a nostalgia
For "The Super-Cigars of Perry White"
I wanted a full run of *Kid Colt*
And needed to do research on Davy Crockett
And Buck Jones of Alkali City.
Heartsick I was for the pile of mags given us
Years before by Greg Armstrong's mum to get rid of them,
A whole thick wad I took a greedy first look through
And smelled the ink
In my grandmother's downstairs toilet
While outside a passerby sang a Frankie Laine
Number followed by a Guy Mitchell.

You with your never-read First Editions in glass bookcases
Envy the reader of comics – soon he'll
Stew in his bedroom all weekend with ancient
Treasures from the charity shop, forgetting the existence
Of his Social Security documents, wages
And the whole convoluted machinery
Of Lloyds, Barclays and the Norwich Union.

K M Dersley.

Josephine

Everybody called her Jo
He called her Josephine
He was the only one that did
And he did this not to endear himself to her
Or to amuse her
Or even to annoy her
He didn't care about that
He called her Josephine for himself

I don't know what she made of it
I never asked her

Darren Gray.

Baby Penguins

Ooooh
Baby Penguins
Ooooooh Ooh
Baby baby penguins
How I luv ya
Oooh
Raised by your fathers
on brave feet
shielded from an
icy death
in the winter blizzard
raised to do the
same again
Its the circle of life
like those lions
only colder
and with flippers
Oooooh
Baby baby penguins
by this writing
I salute you
Oooh.

Lee Nelson.

Forbidden Love

He an active member of the
Sound of Music Appreciation Society
Wearing hand knitted cardigans with pockets
And cosy fleece lined tartan slippers.

She campaigning for the legalisation
Of cannabis for recreational purposes
Dyes her hair bright orange wears
Army fatigues and has one pierced nipple.

They are in love, meeting
Alternative Tuesday afternoons
At an out of town Travel Lodge.

After which, exhausted but happy,
She enjoying a post-coital spliff, he
Listening to Edelweiss on headphones.

Knowing whenever they meet on the street
They must acknowledge each other with
Nothing more than a few disapproving tut-tuts.

David Gildner.

Chrissie Williamson.

'the tree of life'

on a saturday, at 2,
2 at the tree
the monkeys start to gather
around the tree
in milton keynes
i go there
for i am a monkey-minion
sometimes we dance
around the tree
in milton keynes
but security threatens us
with guns
and rabid dogs
so we stop dancing
but the little children always
(and i mean ALWAYS!)
run around the tree
(the magic tree)
(in milton keynes)
with no thought for the saplings
they are careless
but nobody stops them
so we threaten to eat them
kinda heroic in my opinion
but people at the tree
they give us dirty looks
for we are dirty monkeys

Anon.

Desk-Top-Publishing
(the beginners guide to the alphabet)

A is for eight
B is for
C is for sea
E is for aether
F is for phone
G is for jesus
H is for aitchbone
I is for eye
J is for gender
K is for quay
L is for elephant
M is for eminem
N is for envelope
O is for aubergine
Q is for cue
R is for aaaaaaaaaah!
S is for estimate
U is for eureka
V is for weimar
W is for double you
X is for ex boy/girlfriend (delete as appropriate)
Y is for why?
Z is for xylaphone

Lucy Van Pelt.

Ugly's Last Love Song

...was was was
<I Mean, , , I Saw A Video Of You Last Night>
<The You Before There Was We>
<I Mean>
<The You Before I Knew You>

<I Remember When First We>
<When We First>
<You Used To Blink A Lot>
...was was
<Blinking There ; ; ; Nervously>

<Now The You The Me The We>
<And Time Has Gone And Passed Along>
<You Hardly Blink At All>
<And I Mean>
(That It Makes Me Feel)
<To Feel That I Have Made You Feel>
<I Mean To Say>

<I Never Thought That I Would Feel>
<I Feel That I Have Done **Some Good**>
<I Have Made Someone Feel>
<I Mean>

<That It Is That Which I Mean To Say>
<The That That The You The Me The We Can Be>
<I Mean>

<Oh>
<I Mean>

...was
<I Mean>

<That It Is>
<That It Is>
<That Is What I Mean>

That It Is ...

matthew michael taylor.

Anyone for a game of hangman?

_ h _ _ _

Paul Grant.

:BLACK

Time

Time doesn't pass
It bloody well sticks around
Taking itself

Time doesn't pass
It hogs all the days
Selfishly

Time doesn't pass
It fails

Time doesn't heal either.

Gay.

Starved

It was your star sign and it killed you.
There are easier ways to learn things you said.
Of course there are.
Sitting at my brother's window looking out through the curtains.
Red with white clouds drifting down them.
I trace the patterns in the heavens. The animals wink at me.
I believed then that I was not alone.
That light could eat itself for breakfast, lunch, and dinner.
Suck the Milky Way through a straw.
You couldn't get enough sugar.

He told me I was no good as a substitute mother.
The spaghetti sauce splashing on the table.
I knew he didn't know how right he was.
I make the phone calls mechanically.
One rented home after another.
No room at the inn. No hospital beds.
The car window smashed.
He said he couldn't understand breaking things for the fun of
it.
But I could.
Is anger genetic?
A deep rich seam of lost fathers and black holes.

Opening the fridge and asking what there is to eat.
What is behind the wall at the end of the universe?
The great dinner party in the sky.
You'll eat what's on your plate.
The clock folding in on itself.
Cutting the pieces smaller and smaller.
Hidden in the brussels sprouts. The pointlessness of all this
nutrition.
Wandering up and down the aisles to music with the words
    removed.
The elevator tinkle of lost space travellers.
A trip to the supermarket on the moon.

Can you tell this isn't real meat?
The soya protein of another light year. Time frozen or canned.

Not allowed to leave the house without dinner inside you.
I ate the sky and it was delicious.
Popsicles in the heart of winter.
I forget their names now. The constellations I thought were edible.
Loneliness is just another hunger.
That you of all people should starve to death.
There are easier ways. Of course there are.

Aoife Mannix.

the pole-dancer and the crematorium

she's there in the crematorium
with her
fish-net thighs
smouldering eyes
shimmering skin

bumping and grinding she works her art
caskets and coffins
trundling down conveyors
to ash and evermore

to grim epitaphs and stifled yawns
she thrusts
amid sombre faces and serious tones
she slides
un-noticed by mourner and preacher alike

each moment drawing us closer
each breath revealing more

until

at last

furnace door gaping
inferno surrounding
i am consumed

Wayne Miller.

clapham junction

the stale-carpet-breeze pads
across my lips
children with petrol eyes
and uniformed, ragged mice
lights bleach out the navy smother
and i feel a little more contented
nose wrinkling
at urined air and patchy leaks
my aching arms can raise
friends faces in a split twinge
concrete's limp death cold seeps through my coat
they all dance/spar around each other as they wait
and my coffee sours.

Rachel George.

I don't wanna be your friend

I don't wanna be your friend
I don't want niceness
I don't wanna be your friend
I don't want politeness
I don't want to go back
To a life that's dull
A life that's empty
And vice less
I don't wanna be your friend
I can't just turn off my feelings
I can't let go of history
And all my secret yearnings

I don't wanna be your friend
I don't want texts
Saying " Hi hw ws Ur dy? "
I want sleazy phone sex
A list of deliciously filthy
Things you want to do with me
And when we do meet up *I want us do them all*
Thoroughly
I don't want a peck on the cheek
And polite hugging
I want hungry tongues
And inappropriate touching
I want us not to care
Where we are and who's watching
I want to disgust the assistants
When we go out shopping
I want your hand on my groin
While your Mum serves up food
I want oral sex when she nips to the shops
We were always in the mood
I want lust and longing
That never ends
I want my old lover back
I don't wanna be your friend

I want it to be obvious to everyone

That we're a pair
I want us to go back to doing everything together
Everywhere
I don't want to ride the bus
To my house all alone
I want to embarrass a taxi driver
As he chauffeurs us home
I want us getting undressed
Before we even reach the door
I want sweaty humping
Right there on the floor
I want long slow
Lasting lovemaking
I want hectic fucking
Till the walls are quaking
I don't want the *"honeymoon"* period
Ever to end
I want us to go on forever
I don't wanna be your friend

I want to wake naked and shivering
In the wee small hours
Being careful not to wake you
As I claw back the covers
Drifting off to sleep listening to
Calm even breathing
Lingering too long over goodbyes
When it comes to leaving
I wanna bask in the warmth
Of what it is to be near you
Hugging and snuggling
Missing not being with you
It's friendship that turns into Love
Not the opposite
You turn me on and I can't turn off
No matter how much I might try it
I've got enough I don't need anymore
I hate this emotional dead end
I've room in my life for a lover
But *I can't just go on being your friend*

Paul Rafferty.

A drowning girl

Shy pale water will take her far
far away, beyond the lily and the bones
bare bones of the shipwreck, naked fingers
fingers of calcified coral, and her hair
her hair slowly explodes.
Cold mist will hide her body, her eyes
eyes that fishlike penetrate the waves
she waves, her limbs a pale and twisting puppet
a puppet, a swastika, a cross, a slowly
slowly sinking propeller.
Dark and gradual calming of the watery
watery grave will take the red
red lips down to the silt and the body
to bodies who reach up from the golden
golden barrows to seize her hands.
Her ceremonial descent ends with the kiss
soft kiss of salty rot and the bonelike
christlike she whispers Ophelia, Lusitania,
her body begins to echo down the river

Andi Thomas.

: The Bauhaus Style

1960s:
The American Embassy in Athens
Attacked

She now defines her husband W -
Her husband's death - incuriously

Until he becomes given. A measured
Feature of postmodern architecture -

A fixed post driven deep
Into hardened earth to mark
The edges of something

Painful, irrevocable and extant -

Like Walter Gropius arriving
At Harvard with his luggage.

She tells everyone the same thing
Again and again
                        but each time
It becomes a little different -

Less and less
The man who fled
And more the man
Who almost returned -

Textiles, glass and socialism
Socialism, textiles and glass

Democracy. Light and Dark -

Her husband falling backwards

Backwards

    through time and space
cracking his skull wide open
    on the cold marble floor
of his own museum.

Steven Taylor.

Pelt

Keep clawing
at the edge of the
pit; the mud; the ledge;
the thawing grit...

Your dream -
to bubble, blood and spit -
to be the fox -
to be the trouble,
lit as if by torchlight.

Late,
and seeing double.
Snow. And rocks.
I'll get my shovel.

matthew michael taylor.

You Bring Me Rainbows

I am a dark
Deep
Pool of oil
With far flung shores
Just black
Dark black
Deep black
With far flung shores

You stand solitary on one of those shores
And toss marbles
Of all colours
Iridescent colours
Into the black
Dark black
Deep black
With far flung shores

Splash! Ripples
And in those ripples
The sun is caught
Waves of light
You bring me rainbows
To ride
To climb
Liquid walls of colour

And the marbles sink
In to the black
Deep, dark black
With far flung shores
The surface calms
But the marbles lay below
Still as bright
And I still feel the ripples
And I still see the waves of light

Darren Gray.

Poem Written After 'the Dream Life of Angels'.

It was the first day
of a new job
and I'd just filled
the pallet with boxes.
I asked the lad
next to me what we
did next.
He pointed to the empty
pallet that had replaced
the first, then pointed
back at the conveyor.

When I got home
I went straight
up the stairs to bed.
That night in my sleep
the pallets and boxes
returned over
and over
as the nightmares
that stopped me
from dying.

Neil Campbell.

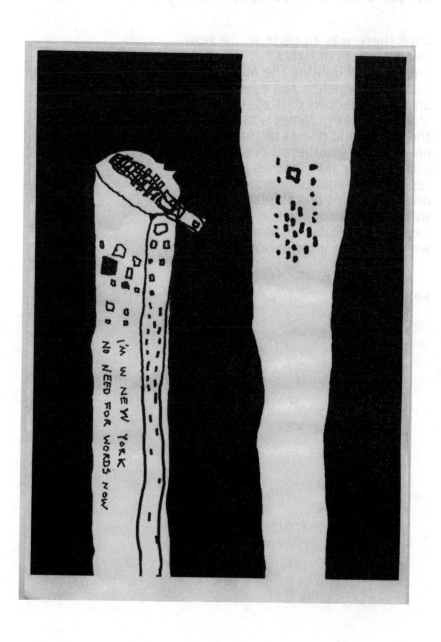

Louise Fowler.

207

where are the white lights

once there was an eerie white glow
small pockets of lights ;
measles highlighting the alleys
haunting shapeless red eyes
unknown shadows cast against walls
Shelley, Stoker, James and Edgar
the spirits and ghosts of the imagination.
now we are smothered in orange
polluting our skin, houses and souls
repressed sexuality in underpaths
drunken scraps on roundabouts
suffocated in copper hue
Easton Ellis, Robert Baker and Irvine
we need little imagination for horror.

Selena Kyle.

The New-Improved Manifesto of the Post-Liberal Malcontents

* We've been living here forever and we're sick of it.

* I walk past upstairs windows in the glow of the night where moonlight licks the lamps. I am music as a gas, chew the time from my chords. In one mouth and out the other. I am disposable, twinkling, plastic trash. Bostik for romantics.
I am cold. My eyes are sore.

* When I take my shirt off I have this knife taped to my belly that she hasn't seen before. She is disappointed and she turns away.

* We are leaving and I wet myself. I dream that I am home.

* I am living at the house on poo corner. I am all alone here. I am living here and I don't like it.

* Sometimes we get excited. Sometimes we get upset.
We eat all the sweets then there's nothing left.

* Evening comes soft in the house on poo corner. It's hot, dog days, and the doo doo rises, rank and steaming, gaseous into the air. Sickly smiles of sun coloured delicate limeade by the beeches carry the cloy of the cack into this room with my books and records. This used to be the nice end of town. This is where when I always lived live wherever I went go. Poetry, atmosphere. Do you get it now ? Why and all that ?

* We've been living here forever and we're sick of it.

* Anyway, I also have a kitchen and I eat sausages with instant mash and beans. I drink orange squash. In the street outside I now have a car. I only drive it late at night and I never drive above second gear. I love to get a big queue stuck behind me on a narrow road.

* I am living with my mother in the house I grew up in. I have

209

a different bedroom now to the one I had as a child because when I moved out of here the first time my mother sealed up my old room to preserve it as it was when I was at home. She has had a glass panel set into the door so she can look in without entering. She dusts once a week wearing white gloves. Sometimes I sneak a look in through the glass. I can see my dressing gown hanging on the bed-end where I left it.

* I am living here. I don't like it. Not one little bit. People don't really respond when I'm with them. People don't really care if I phone them. People don't listen when I speak to them. People ring me up then pretend to be someone else. I haven't got a television licence. People send me photos of myself in funny places looking stupid. I haven't seen people for weeks. I don't think we get on.

* What to do in case of fire :
Walk towards flames until heat becomes too great or death results. If relevant, retire to a safe distance, focus the mind, practice pain resistance techniques, approach flames again. Repeat unto death.
What to do if the land is devastated by a flash flood of the milk of human kindness :
Piss in it then build a boat.
What to do if someone approaches you in the spirit of friendship :
Kick them hard where it hurts and let them see the glint in your eye as they double up.

* It's all a fucking con. On every level and on every level are we screwed. Once you realise what a twisted joke everything EVERYTHING is then you go mad, die, or laugh and merrily walk away and cling to the things you cling to. There is hope but it is so unsatisfying. There is death but it is joyously deluded. Give me shitty fucked-up western values shafted by the redundant corpse of the Pope or give me death.

* I have to keep on like this, talking. If I don't I'll start seeing things again. Sorry no poem, all my poems are shit. I'd rather be beaten unconscious with the severed cock of a chimpanzee than read one out.

Lee Nelson.

Poem that summarises much of Walt Whitman without all the airy-fairy angst-ridden waffle.

Death
is like that little light inside your fridge,
only bigger.

Alice Nemo.

211

THE YOUNG POET AND HIS PALS VISIT ... Nash

A small village just outside the current boundaries of MK, where Jim grew up, early 2003.

In the earlier half of the last century, you see, there were other small rural and farming villages around here like Nash. Surrounded by fields, rolling hills and copses of woods for a few miles at a time, until the next little village broke the countryside. Their names? Places like Bradwell, Loughton and Woolstone.

Now, of course, they nestle among red-bricked estates and grid roads, swallowed by the red brick city as it grows and grows. And although Nash seems like a long way out into the countryside in 2003 (it's four miles south of Stony, three miles west of Bletchley – but the roads out thataway twist and wind all over), plans are still afoot to extend Milton Keynes over the coming decades. And that's the likely direction it's gonna go...

So, standing in Nash, which is on a relatively high plateau, you can look out across the fields and see the city coming. It has special resonance for Jim, he spent much of his youth here, and he's filled with nostalgia as we amble around the streets of the village (always walking on the right hand side of the road to face the coming traffic – that's the country code!)

His Nan still lives there, in fact, and our journey really starts in her kitchen, as she makes us both a cup of tea before we go out into the briskly cold January afternoon. Like all proper Nan Kitchens, it's full of ornaments, and I found it enormously reassuring.

There are two halves to Nash, Jim tells me as we walk, the gentryfolk farmers, and the workers who staff the farms. Which is why one part of the village is council houses, a larger part is sprawling farmsteads. The air is often redolent with the classic smell of British silage. The occasional posh looking dog wanders about.

Some of the houses, in fact, are massive – but on closer inspection many of them have been newly built. There must be a whole class of MK citizens who live out here in the hinterlands, able to pop over to the city in their four-wheel drive jeeps. There are far more houses here than farms now, so even now the village is growing.

I wonder what it must be like growing up in such a place. Haversham, where I did, is in the first countryside north of the city, but a ten minute walk and you're in Wolverton. Plus there's a bus every hour to the city centre. In Nash, there are three buses every day, and Jim says that's a massive improvement since his youth. But, boy, it's quiet here.

Yet also there is history. In a small graveyard by a quiet countryside church, lie several of Jim's forebears. We wander around, respectfully trying to tread in the right places, and I start to contemplate the nature of the present. Less and less do families stay in the same place for generations – particularly true of Milton Keynes, of course, where the majority of families have been here only a generation at best...

What will this place turn into if the city grows out this way? Jim and meself went to a Council Meeting affair just before Christmas where lots of different people talked about the expansion of Milton Keynes. We do try and take this journalism thing seriously sometimes, y'know. And before that meeting, it hadn't even occurred to me that the continuing growth of the city might be A Bad Thing.

I had always just thought – "Yay, MK!!! Keep on growing bigger and bigger till we're the new capital of England!!!". But, of course, that's a bit of a naïve attitude. Did you notice?

It turns out that the issue is forced on the local council by central government – John Prescott wants MK to grow, so boy, it growing. However, the myriad of different environmental groups at this Meeting affair didn't seem to be so keen. Which was an eye-opener to say the least, although like most of my discoveries, it seems obvious when you think about it. The bigger the city grows, the more problems that will entail. Wits will have to be kept about us. And when does it stop?

Will Nash get it's own set of Greenleys shops to hang around outside? Will there be more red bricks among the country lanes? Who knows. I'm just a poet. Sleep tight. Don't have nightmares...

A Night In May

I can taste blood in my mouth
spit it out as I try
not to be sick
there, always there
present
at the back of my mind
telling me
I'm wrong
so here is my regret
I won't do it again

Caz Wolfson.

after grandpa's death

they
came in.

and could not have performed
any better than maggots whirling in old meat,
they stripped grandpa's garage down:

took all his drills and hammers,
they took his gas compressor and lathe,
they took and took to support their short-term needs

where just to borrow was not enough

but took and took

and when grandma asked me what I wanted
I shook my head,
thinking that the memories were enough:
my first car as a birthday present - an 1100 Morris
and some conversation from him about a war that was not a
good idea to
forget.

but I did take the 3 pairs of socks
grandma offered me
and I still wear
one pair now

Brad Evans.

Her First and Second Husbands

An old schoolfriend of my mother
had a husband and three young kids.
One morning, aged thirty-seven,
he went out to get the milk bottles,
had a heart attack and died.
My mother's friend took twenty years
to marry again.
When she did, it was to a kindly chap
in his early seventies.
After five years of happy marriage,
she woke to find him dead,
more conventionally,
in their marital bed.

Again, the day's milk curdled in the sun.

Kevin Densley.

Mr Bread

Mr Bread is a regular informant
Always reliable, rarely wrong.
Mr Bread sniffs out Nazis for us.
Mr Bread searches the yellow pages on a daily basis,
Looking for tell-tale Nazi symbolism.

Mr Bread peeps out of his window
And calls us if he sees anyone
    goosestepping up Elm Street.
Or fitting Hitler's description.

Mr Bread uses complex ciphers to
    weed out Nazis from the telephone book.
Mr Bread knows where you live.
He's got your number.
He called us 15 minutes ago,
Fritzy boy.

Simon Edwards.

Amie-May.

Self Aware

To drop below the surface and see beyond the horizon.

You must hold your breath.

Images of feathers awaken you to sunrise
and rain falls through your hair.

Because.

You can honestly say that you like the look of chrome.
Doesn't it feel somehow false? An illusion that is hard.

To release.

Crystalline texture and igneous rock lay like sediment on the floor.
Who will pick up the pieces? A tedious job.

Can make you.

Broken shards and British weather do so much. Soon we become.

Homo sapient.

Wayne Miller.

Mindtrap

Chasing a pot of fictional gold
At the end of my evaporating rainbow of hope,
Made of light caught, held in the moment.

Never really there.

Disappointment floods my heart again
A torrential downpour of despair,
Creating a dull grey reality.

I'm the kid who lost their balloon
Dropped their ice cream
Ruined their party dress.

Messed up their life
By hoping too much.

The scales have fallen off my eyes.
I can see the grey concrete blocks
 that put parameters on my life.

Reality pierces my skull,
diamond bullet style.
And I see how far I can really run on these legs.

Amelia Stubberfield.

Cruciate Ligament Injury

Strangely fixed together
Chewing gum and sellotape
Skin replaced with leather
One side for hurt one side for hate

We kissed you yesterday
Try to stop you asking why
You will always look away
Before you look me in the eye

Sometime say it. Sometimes say it. Sometimes just say it.
You're not half the man you used to be.
I'm not half the man I used to be.

Keith Crawford.

Studying war poetry, again

Once more into the bleak,
picking apart the blood-stained poppies
and pinning them to a tired parade of how the west was won.
Back to the old arguments.
Considering style and substance, pondering inspiration,
Taking an inexpertly wielded scalpel to the long-dead;
Pessimism and patriotism and polemic; protest and poignancy
and Petrarch.
Inwardly weeping at the downright beautiful.
Sitting in the classroom, all at once, we seize the edge of the
scab and heave,
The rush of pain is instant, and then it ebbs away,
We look down, hoping to see healed and pink new skin, but our
hearts sink, And blood gushes onto the cold floor.
Of course we all want to know what he meant, what she was
trying to say;
But I think I'll draw the line at a bullet in my head
The reverence is punctuated with giggles, as the classroom
reasserts itself.
We lock the ghosts back into the book, with their flickering
candles and tolling bells,
The mists retreat. The room's a little lighter round the edges
now.
The shared sideways glances glitter edgily above unsure smiles;
The words on the page shrink back down:
Cross-shaped shadows melt away beneath the daylight.
Now the muddy blood of bleeding youth is just another peg
For rhyme, rhythm, metre; for academic progress.
But the hollow gloss we receive comes from a pyrite chalice
And splutters in our throat, shakes once, and dies.
Perhaps we can be forgiven for the speed with which
We leave that shaky place. Talking too loudly.
For a fleeting second I'd begun to quiver, my stomach turned
to lice,
And a million million dead men marched behind my eyes.

Andi Thomas.

daddylonglegsseason

the evenings roll on in, the nights are bland.
we sit on different sofas to pretend
that this is not another like the last.
by ten o'clock the three of us feel stunned.

the kitchen is alive with tiny legs.
i brave them while i'm looking for her fags.
they fizz into the danger of the bulb
and rest upon the slow congealing mugs.

i count up all my change to get some beer.
the wax inside my lamp is knotted fire.
we turn off all the lights so we'll be safe,
but the buzzing/humming screen becomes a lure.

the smoke has curled a layer round our feet;
we mutter as The Fear begins to start.
our trainers crush their frail insect lives.
i fall asleep again, still in my coat.

my mouth is full of wet Doritos scum.
across the walls they flitter scutter skim.
i wish that they had never got inside.
will this insipid winter never come?

matthew michael taylor.

Since she turned remote.

She used to come to me
and turn the control
till silence was gone.
But now she keeps a
comfortable distance.
I hardly feel the brush
of fingers, merely
the thick coats
of desire's dust
and the occasional
kicks of hope, now
my only pleasure
the sweet revenge
of fuzzy pictures
and missed episodes,
her faults my only solace
since she turned remote.

John G Hall.

brine shrimp

discuss raising the freeze-dried creatures
That's why we made a culture out of "Fun" and "Nothing"
You'll laugh your simian tale off
We've got the "real" thing (as real as they get)
the official NOTHING of the millennium
I think I saw this cloning with a box of sea monkeys thrown in.
don't give them bananas -
they may be monkeys but they will be
suffocated by the large banana in their little tank

K T.

Without being culpably particular

Like the snowed in cake under icing sugar,
Your head
Lay back, and dropped-rope slack
Your neck, on sleep-flat pillows on
Your bed
Run with yellow veins and cracked
Like leather, your legs crossed, your
Mouth hung, your limbs freezing slowly,
Grandad, you're dead.
And I kiss your clammy, plastic
Forehead
As I did yesterday, before I said
That it was getting late and you should go
To bed.

Rachel George.

Cheap Suits

We are the *people in the* cheap suits
Mr.Byrite, Man & Woman at *C&A*
We are the *people in the* cheap suits
We're packed, we're ready, we're on our way
We've pens and paper and clipboards
And forms to fill up and down
We want your name on the dotted line
And we are in your town
With too much stubble, acne and make-up
Badly bleached hair with fading roots
We're gonna tick you all off 'cos
We are the *people in the* cheap suits

You can tell by the tone of our shirts
You can tell by the cut of our voices
We've got a cause, we take no prisoners
And we offer no clear choices
We're on your doorstep
We're on a mission
It's just how we live our lives
No basic – *all commission*
So we comb our hair
And spit on our shoes
And get ready to make an offer
That you just *can't refuse*

'Cos
We are the *people in the* cheap suits
And we're raring to go
We are the *people in the* cheap suits
We don't hear the word *"No"*
"Are you happy with your windows?"
"Have you considered draught proofing?"
"How much are your heating bills?"
And *"How secure is your roofing?"*
"Is this your daughter?
What a pretty dress
I've spoken to your neighbours
And they all said 'Yes'"

"Are you getting your full discount?"
"Can I offer you a bribe?"
"We picked your house out of thousands
Could I please just step inside?"
Double glazing, Triple glazing
"Your own personal Piece of Mind"
A cheaper gas option
"If you would just be so kind
As to sign away for a year and a day
On a two week rolling contract"
If you change your mind – we still get paid
And you can get'cha money back
"How safe are your valuables?"
"How cosy is your loft?"
And *"How can you resist?"*
When the hard sell starts so *soft*
A creeping tide of politeness
Breaking over suburban shoots
Just crush them underfoot while you open the door
To *the people in the* cheap suits

Paul Rafferty.

WWI through V

World War I was great
World War II was the war to end all wars
World War III almost finished us
World War IV was virtual
World War V was a dream I had
When I awoke my coffee was cold
And I don't even drink coffee

Darren Gray.

come on die young

so scared that it will leave me
so scared that through my fingertips
i'll feel it melt away,
but i savour the moment
more than words can say
for This is the Beautiful Sound
i feel it pulse through my veins
i feel my heart beat so hard
i feel myself falling,
i hold my breath
it slips away,
and Listen to the Beautiful Sound
it smothers me, twisting around
so soft and sound, past littered ground
and it makes me glad that i can hear
and it makes me glad to be alive
for a spellbound moment
blinking tears from my eyes
i Hear only the Beautiful Sound
it sends a shiver down my spine,
too much feeling, few words sung
and i am happy
and i am content,
and i know for once that i belong
with the beautiful sound
all is not gone
it sighs
<come on...
die young...>

Lucy Van Pelt.

For Ian

There's a light
that's shining somewhere here,
perhaps beyond the shadow's boundary.
I'm still searching
for something near.
I can't see it
I can't see it.

There's a bell
that's sounding close to me,
perhaps in silence I will hear it.
Strain to hear it
quietly.
I'm listening
I'm listening.

There's a hand
that I was holding tight,
just to pass the squeeze around us.
It must be there
just beyond the light.
I'm reaching
I'm reaching.

There's something absent
from this picture.
I must have lost it in the winter.
Where is the ending
to this story?
I can't find it
I can't find it.

Dave Stephenson.

memorial for a man

I can wake up
yawn
smile to myself knowing that
I am missed
evidence from a message
sent when I was sleeping
he, however
will not wake up
nor open his eyes to the
morning sun
but will be sorely missed
untimely ripped from
this world
once, we sat here,
laughed
but he lost his voice
a week has passed
how have they coped?
and the future, what of that?
never forgotten
but too cruel.
how can you smile God,
when this is all the protection
you give us?
how can the Religious claim
it was his time
and carry on, knowing
they have forever for their goodness?
but, was he not good too?
loved and lost
there is no justice
and no reason.
we will rage
and clamour for
the past
we will clad ourselves
in cotton wool
and hide our loved ones
God cannot play with life

in such a careless manner
emotions will pour onto a page
through spoken words
absorbed by the mourners
but nothing will reach him
the sun's rays are not strong enough:
as weak as he was
before he surrendered
they will linger
bathe us in hope of
a new day
where we will remember,
wake up and yawn
but have a greater value for life
and quietly defy God
with every day we stay alive

for jon, 16/12/82 - 09/03/03

Caz Wolfson.

MONKEY KETTLE: A MILTON KEYNES COUNTER-CULTURE WAITING FOR A CULTURE

MONKEY KETTLE HAVE BEEN EATING + + + +

A special anthology of the very tastiest morsels from the groaning table at Monkey Kettle Towers over the past five years... The Soundtrack To Our Lives, basically!

BOOKS

"Microserfs" by Douglas Coupland // "Five Go To Smuggler's Top" by Enid Blyton // "The Gormenghast Trilogy" by Mervyn Peake // "Everything: A Book About Manic Street Preachers" by Simon Price // "The Modern Antiquarian" by Julian Cope // "Lives Of The Poets" by Michael Schmidt // "The Swish Of The Curtain" by Pamela Brown // "Moab Is My Washpot" by Stephen Fry // "The Amazing Adventures Of Kavalier And Clay" by Michael Chabon // "The Dark Tower Series" (1 - 5 so far) by Stephen King // "House Of Leaves" by Mark Z.Danielewski // "Oscar Wilde" by Richard Ellman // "On The Road" by Jack Kerouac // "The Long Walk" by Richard Bachman // "The Age Of Reason" by Jean-Paul Sartre // "The Quarrel Of The Age" by A C Grayling // "The Miracle Of Castel di Sangro" by Joe McGinniss // "His Dark Materials" trilogy by Philip Pullman // "The Dante Club" by Matthew Pearl // "A Star Called Henry" by Roddy Doyle //

MUSAK

"Everything Picture" by Ultrasound // "The Fidelity Wars" by Hefner // "Joined Up Talking" by My Life Story // "Spit" by Kittie // "Way To Blue" by Nick Drake // "The Marshall Mathers LP" by Eminem // "Rated R" by Queens Of The Stone Age // "Gorillaz" by Gorillaz // "Origin Of Symmetry" by Muse // Moulin Rouge Soundtrack // "The Moldy Peaches" by The Moldy Peaches // "Run Come Save Me" by Roots Manuva // "The Coral" by The Coral // "Original Pirate Material" by The Streets // "White Blood Cells" by The White Stripes // "Permission To Land" by The Darkness // "Absolution" by Muse // "You Can Feel Me" by Har Mar Superstar // "A Grand Don't Come For Free" by The Streets // "The Futureheads" by The Futureheads

FILM

"Grosse Pointe Blank" (1997, dir.George Armitage) // "The Blair Witch Project" (1999, dir.Daniel Myrick & Eduardo Sánchez) // "South Park : Bigger Longer & Uncut" (1999, dir.Trey Parker) // "Being John Malkovich" (2000, dir.Spike Jonze) // "High Fidelity" (2000, dir.Stephen Frears) // "Memento" (2000, dir.Christopher Nolan) // "Billy The Kid And The Green Baize Vampire" (1985, dir.Alan Clarke) // "Twin Peaks : Fire Walk With Me" (1992, dir.David Lynch) // "Moulin Rouge" (2001, dir.Baz Luhrmann) // "The Castle" (1997, dir.Rob Sitch) // "Lord Of The Rings : Fellowship Of The Ring" (2001, dir.Peter Jackson) // "Shaolin Soccer" (2001, dir Stephen Chow & Lik-Chi Lee) // "Wonder Boys" (2000, dir.Curtis Hanson) // "Series 7 : The Contenders" (2001, dir.Daniel Minahan) // "8 Mile" (2002, dir.Curtis Hanson) // "Adaptation" (2002, dir.Spike Jonze) // "Combat Academy" (1986, dir.Neal Israel) // "Lord Of The Rings : Return Of The King" (2003, dir.Peter Jackson) // "Lost In Translation" (2003, dir.Sofia Coppola) // "Eternal Sunshine Of The Spotless Mind" (2004, dir.Michel Gondry) // "Chopper" (2000, dir.Andrew Dominik) // "Finding Neverland" (2004, dir.Marc Foster) //

MISCELLANEOUS

The Tray Game : sport of champions // Pokémon // Christina Ricci // Eating Southern Fried Chicken on Hunstanton Beach on a very cold day // The Jimi Volcano Quintet // Campbell Park at 4.30am // Big Brother 1 : "he who lives by the sword dies by the sword" // 75% Lip // League of Gentlemen // down the dogs // Evenings of Diverse Entertainment // Paolo di Canio's goal to knock Man Utd out of the FA Cup at Old Trafford (28.01.01) // falling off JCBs into the mud // Ludamus Theatre Company (Here Be Monsters, Papanuwenwe, The Block And The Wire, Pirates) // Kitchen darts // Hide and seek // Spaced // John Hegley, twice // Jackass // Archaeology evening class at Stantonbury // Andrews Liver Salts // CMK Library // Oceana // Paperfish // Michael Palin // Tony doing 'Krapp's Last Tape' at MADCAP, twice // Day trip to York – "I saw some terrible things in 'Nam" // William Hazlitt // HitchHikers' Guide To The Galaxy radio series // The West Wing // The Silmarillion on tape // Kerguelen // Hollyoaks Ban // Fifteen Storeys High // Broadband // Doom, Doom 2 and Final Doom // RIP John Peel, a true hero //

BIOGS : You Have Been Watching

CISSY AEON
Cissy has recently been absent from the world of literature due to a severe swelling of her procrastination gland. She is currently convalescing in hospital and would welcome visits from anyone who is willing to feed her grapes or cut up her dinner for her.

AMIE-MAY
"There's nothing wrong with looking more lived, those smiling wrinkles are becoming more prominent, even more so now mini me has been born. Thankyou Monkey Kettle, I'm enriched and some would say redeemed."

BUNNY
suitable for those under 36 months, all staples and razor blades removed.

NEIL CAMPBELL
lives in Manchester and writes poems and short stories.

SIMON CHAMBERS
I am an artist. I paint mostly but every once in a while I write a little something. Just doing my bit to help keep the world turning.

TOM CHAPMAN
Tom was too busy dreaming about big, red, fast space rockets (ones that go to the moon and have ray guns and stuff) to think up a decent bio.

MIKE CORDELL
(to be read in the style of Glen A. Larson):
From the heart of darkness comes a man who does not exist.

A bleak soul astride a black steed. His boots are soiled, but he has scrubbed them well, and few shall remember his passing.

KEITH CRAWFORD

a verbatim text message :"I live with five beautiful girls, am being courted with multi-million pound contracts by international law firms, and spend most of my mornings throwing up. You?"

CAROLINE DAVIES

Caroline Davies has been writing poetry for twenty years but still regards herself as a beginner, especially when confronted with a blank page.

KEVIN DENSLEY

Kevin Densley lives in Melbourne, Australia. His poetry has appeared in various Australian publications, including Quadrant, Adelaide Review, Space, Verandah and Mattoid - and numerous UK magazines including Other Poetry, Monkey Kettle, The Journal and Cadenza. He also writes plays (with Steve Taylor). These have been performed Australia-wide. Densley and Taylor have co-authored nine books and one CD-Rom – mainly play collections for young people. His latest book is the play Last Chance Gas, published by Currency Press, Sydney, in 2003.

K M DERSLEY

Poems and articles by K.M. Dersley have been appearing since 1974 in such magazines as Poetry Review, London Magazine and The Rialto. His books include Sketches by Derz (stories & articles) and Between the Alleyways at the World's Fair (poems). He has performed his work in London, Cambridge, Colchester, Chelmsford, Ipswich, at the Wessex Festival and at 2003's Dulwich Festival where he sang and played guitar as well as reading. In June 2000 KMD launched his website The Ragged Edge (**www.raggededge.btinternet.co.uk**) for his own outpourings. Then he started including the work of other writers in it on 'The Other Side of the Ragged Edge.'

RACHEL DILLON
Rachel left MK several years ago to experience the Welsh way of life, but has recently returned to the fold in order to teach young children the wonders of the world. She has very little spare time, but when she does, she reads, writes, travels and socialises avidly.

SIMON EDWARDS
Simon Edwards is the best poet in this book. If you buy one book of poetry for £10 this year buy six copies of "Captain Gin" and send him the change, if you buy two publications, buy this book as well but just read his bits.

ANTHONY KANE EVANS
Conceived in Manchester. Shot in Sunderland. Edited in Newcastle. Colour corrected in Copenhagen. Now showing in Monkey Kettle. Makes music videos, video spots for conferences and occasional documentaries for Danish television. His first short story appeared in the anthology Signals 3 (London Magazine Editions) back in 2001.

BRAD EVANS
Brad Evans was born in Sydney, 1971. His poems, articles, interviews, short stories, letters and reviews have been published in over a hundred zines, magazines (printed / online) and anthologies throughout Europe, the U.S., Canada, and Australia. His first full-length book of poems, 'and them and the jackals and the night', was privately published in March 2001. Brad is also the founder and editor of the print and online journal, Red Lamp, a journal that publishes realist, socialist and humanitarian poetry: **www.geocities.com/red_lamp**. An audio CD of this journal's launch, featuring working class poetry from the inaugural issue, is also available. Aside from poetry and prose, Brad also writes filmscripts for short films.

LOUISE FOWLER
is an Illustrator from Cornwall. She draws things that happen inside Heads.

241

JO GALLOWAY
I have an eclectic mind developed over 40 + years which is reflected in my writing. For me, poetry is word art, as I cannot paint I write, using my paper as canvas and my words as colour. I have been blessed with a complicated life which offers great writing fodder.

MATT GAMBRILL
born and brought up in the south east, i now live on the fringes of the lake district where i spend my free time cutting the heads off daffodils.

GAY
who is and isn't.

RACHEL GEORGE
wachie g likes the following things in order of how much she likes them, not in an arbitrary nonpreferential order : the weakerthans, cheese, not working for luton borough council cleansing customer services. i love you allllll!

DAVID GILDNER
Writes poetry locked away in a crumbling gothic tower, wearing velvet knee britches and a frilly white shirt using just a quill and parchment, His eyesight, eyebrows and toupee all ruined by working to close to a solitary candle. A member of the Open University Poetry Society, who spends his days recalling his lost youth and the past glories of Liverpool Football club and trying not to sound bitter.

PAUL GRANT
Is 28 years old, works as a cleaner, and has lived in MK his whole life.

DARREN GRAY
Raised in the sleepy rural idyll that is Luton, Bedfordshire Darren

had big dreams. Many varied childhood, teenage and early adulthood dramas followed (herculean efforts, wild tempests, struggles to defeat evil in the face of sure annihilation and the like) before he eventually gracefully and gratefully came to rest upon the lip of the old and the new - this glorious New Horizon - Milton Keynes, where he works for the Council. Big dreams. Darren is the author of the very successful "Delicate Eelephant" - ISBN 0-9544-0113-1 - a fantastic accompaniment to any life filled with anything.

STEVE GROOM

is a modern artist, but unfortunately his bicycle is in a desperate need of repair.

DIANE HAINSWORTH

I crashed down on the crossbar and the pain was enough to make a shy, bald Buddhist reflect and plan a mass-murder.

JOHN G HALL

John is a poet from Manchester England. Recent publications include Fire, Coffee House Poetry, Left Curve, the People's Poet Anthology, The Ugly Tree, Current Accounts, The Journal, Running Water, Orbis and is a featured poet in Bewrite books anthology 'Routes' which came out in 2004. He considers himself a lapsed Marxist-Buddhist.

FAITH HOPE

has now struck the thirties. However, she still likes stuff, has a weakness for things, and can often be seen places. For more of the same (but less of that), try http://uk.geocities.com/faithhope69

NIKKI IBBOTSON

Nikki exists but doesn't know why. She stops babies from crying in supermarkets and wishes she was a cartoon character with invincibility powers. She makes music because she likes to, art because she wants to, and mess because she needs to. She lives on a shoestring with a dog and a mouse (rip pico) and has an addiction to all things sweet and chocolatey.

K T
experimental photographer, splits & high kicks. watching the dialing tone.

STEVEN M KENDALL
Steve has lost his biog. He thought he had it in a bag, but he can't find the bag. It might be in the pocket of his other trousers, but they're not here. Oh well. Hello. To be continued...

SELENA KYLE
Thinks celibacy is a polite term for ugly people who can't get laid. Apart from nuns, people without sexual organs, children, priests and possibly people recovering from a bad relationship. Put it this way, if a rabbit says they are celibate, its because they're ugly.

LARD
hippy/tramp/grebo/singer/artist/writer.

THOMAS McCOLL
Top Five Hong Kong movie babes : 1. Michelle Yeoh in "Crouching Tiger Hidden Dragon", 2. Moon Lee in "Angel" and "Dreaming the Reality", 3. Chingamy Yau in "Naked Killer", 4. Amy Yip in "Robotrix" and "Sex and Zen", 5. Maggie Cheung in "Irma Vep".

JULIUS MAN
I must confess I do not have any great manifesto to go with my writing, I simply enjoy reading and writing poems and stories.
I live and work in Cheltenham and have been writing poetry for a number of years. I particularly like Philip Larkin's poetry and Roger McGough's. I like a large number of Sylvia Plath poems too, although a great many of them leave me baffled!

244

AOIFE MANNIX
Aoife Mannix was born in Stockholm, Sweden in 1972, grew up in Dublin and New York, and currently lives in London. Her poetry has been published in First Time magazine, the New Writer, Breathe, Fan The Flames, and Gargoyle #42 as well as being broadcast on BBC Radio 4 and the BBC World Service. In 1998 she was awarded first prize in the Dr Marten's™ New Writers Competition. She is the current Farrago London Slam Champion.

DAVID R MORGAN
Teaches 11 to 19 year olds in Luton. David has also been an arts worker and literature officer and writer-in-residence for education authorities, a prison and a psychiatric hospital (which was the subject of a Channel 4 film Out Of Our Minds).

LEE NELSON
Lee Nelson was born in Luton and ended up in his ancestral East End via Alsager, Crewe, Alsager, Luton, Cobridge, Alsager, Luton, Whalley Range (two weeks), Luton and Wood Green. He has been published in Gargoyle, Pure Filth and Ocelot and has performed in many of the above places as well as Bedford, Camden, Crouch End, Covent Garden and the Glastonbury Festival. He tries to imbue his writing with a sense of place. He teaches drama in Tottenham and is now older than when he wrote these things herein.

ALICE NEMO
does not write poetry. Or biogs.

JON OYSTER
Lives, writes and performs.

ANDY PEARSON
Andy spins tales that crackle and spark on floating bits of tissue. Headquartered in Zargoid, it's not so easy.

J C H POTTS

I am a young writer living in the South East, leading a rather banal suburban life made interesting only by what mischief I can create; by the time of publication I will have begun studying English at university. My chief passions are for James Joyce and the music of The Smiths. Though I have always been an enthusiastic reader and writer, I have not been writing seriously for more than about a year and a half - however I have won prizes in some local competitions, and in the Foyle Young Poets Competition 2003, which spurred me to think I might make something of my work...

PAUL RAFFERTY

Paul Rafferty used to live in the UK's crappest town, but then he moved to Birmingham.

CHARLES P RIES

lives and writes in Milwaukee, Wisconsin. His poems, poetry reviews and short stories have appeared in over seventy print and electronic publications. He is on the board of the Woodland Pattern Book Center in Milwaukee and can be reached at charlesr@execpc.com

CHARLIE SATINE

Filthy Jellyfish needs Peeing on

TRISH SENIOR

rarely gets a visit from the muse but is usually at home with the kettle on ready just in case.

ANDREW SHELLEY

Freelance poet/critic, widely published, currently living in London. Born 1962, educated at Oxford and Cambridge. Doctorate on Samuel Beckett, Research Fellowship. Part-time teaching. Many articles/reviews in academic and literary journals. Individual poetry publications are Peaceworks (The Many Press) and Requiem Tree (Spectacular Diseases). Pamphlet Nervous Meat due out in the States this year.

KATE SILVER
writes, makes jewellery, fills things up with water, and reads books about places she hasn't yet been.

DAVE STEPHENSON
The path of Dave Stephenson's long life takes many turns whic would scarcely be believed even if you were witness to them. A double identity, a soul made bitter by the machinations of his enemies (but now turned to lighter matters), a silver tongue and a heart of pyrite.

ALPOT STROBE
is an unknown quantity of person who has two legs, a heart and a smile. Wombles and small angles unnerve him and he is enthusiastic about you.

AMELIA STUBBERFIELD
Amelia is an arty type, a northerner at heart and therefore a great believer in the healing powers of tea. She spends her time keeping it real with her homedogs and pimping rides... the usual stuff!

matthew michael taylor
Erratic poet, playwright, 30 and editor of MK's premier poetry mag. Career highs so far include having comedy broadcast on E4, play scenes performed at Manchester's Green Room, being singer in the Hot FM Young Pop Act 1993, and being Milton Keynes Young Poet of the Year 1987. None of those are actually quite as impressive as they sound when you get close up. Still, early doors.

STEVEN TAYLOR
was born and brought up in Hyde, near Manchester, and now lives in Kilburn, north London, as the English aspect of an Irish household. He is widely published in magazines and journals, including work in England, Scotland, Wales, Eire, France, Germany, the USA, Australia, Canada and Belgium.

BARRY TEBB

was born in Leeds in 1942. His first collection, 'The Quarrel with Ourselves' was praised by John Carey in 'The New Statesman' and his work was included in the Penguin Anthology, 'Children of Albion'. 'The Lights of Leeds' (Selected Poems) has been recently published by Redbeck Press. He edits 'Poetry Leeds' and 'Literature and Psychoanalysis'.

ANDI THOMAS

MK Poet now living in London.

JAMES TÜRL

Born the illegitimate son of Shane McGowan and Kirsty MacColl, James was raised by Billy Bragg in an organic yurt, where at the age of eighteen he rebelled against his hippie forebears and went on a right wing tirade; introducing poll tax, evicting miners and running over Chinese fellas in a tank. He's now in a loving relationship with Oliver Letwin, living in Thatcher's milk mines teaching Michael Howard to smile.

LUCY VAN PELT

absinthe makes the heart grow fonder.

ROGAN WHITENAILS

For more scatology and pyrotechnical self-pity, visit: www.electromancer.com/artists/rogan_whitenails

CHRISSIE WILLIAMSON

Moved to MK in 1974, and lived with my parents in Stony Stratford. Later got a house in New Bradwell where James (T Türl, MK fans – MMT) was brought up. Unfortunately, I now live in Harlow, Essex, which is similar but not a patch on MK.

CAZ WOLFSON

lives near the Thames. is ashamed to say that despite having visited Melbourne, did not make it to the Neighbours set. Rubbish. ZAP!

WAYNE MILLER
strides through the world in such a way that his large steps can sometimes make the world seem smaller than it actually is. And it is.